Britain's First Socialists

Britain's First Socialists

The Levellers, Agitators and Diggers
of the English Revolution

Fenner Brockway

Q

QUARTET BOOKS

LONDON MELBOURNE NEW YORK

The publishers would like to thank John Walter for compiling the Chronology of
Main Events and the Selected Reading List, and Leslie S.A. Jones for the
Author's Bibliography

First published by Quartet Books Limited 1980
A member of the Namara Group
27 Goodge Street, London W1P 1FD

ISBN 0 7043 2207 2

Phototypeset by Gavin Martin Limited
26-34 Rothschild Street London SE27 0HQ
Printed and bound in Great Britain by
Redwood Burn Limited,
Trowbridge and Esher

Contents

To the memory of H.N. Brailsford,
historian, humanist, activist, his life
devoted to socialist justice and infinite
beauty, and in gratitude for his
The Levellers in the English Revolution,
to which monumental work
much of this book is indebted

ACKNOWLEDGEMENT

I would like to say a word of special
thanks to Dorothy Morris who converted my
difficult calligraphy into clear typescript.

Illustrations

Burford Church, the font *(Walter Scott Picture Library, Bradford)*

Cromwell dissolving the Long Parliament *(Mary Evans Picture Library)*

A selection of contemporary pamphlets appears between pages 142 and 143

Foreword

by the Rt Hon. Tony Benn, M.P.

British history, as it is taught in our schools, is the history of the rich and the powerful and the use they made of their wealth and power. The work and struggles of ordinary folk are mentioned, if at all, mainly to buttress the main story of how the country was governed by the people who controlled the real levers of power.

We are still told very little about the actual working conditions and lives of those who created the wealth by their work in field, factory and office; of their incomes and living standards; of the values they upheld and developed and of the ideas that they evolved as a result of their experience. Yet somehow these unreported factors can be felt to be at work in shaping our attitudes today and will be a powerful force in shaping our future.

Of all the formative influences in the long history of our people, the English Civil War in the seventeenth century is still one of the most important. Under the surface, every Englishman is still a Royalist or a Parliamentarian. And the reason is clear: for it was in that conflict that some of the central issues of politics were fought over and argued through in a way that brought to the fore those who had been held down by the feudal system as William the Conqueror imposed it after 1066.

Looking back three hundred and more years to the events of that period it is astonishing – and deeply satisfying – to note that many of the basic questions which we still debate today were raised and fought over by a group of men and women who called themselves the Levellers and who succeeded in formulating a structure of constitutional ideas that was to become the basis for the French and American revolutionaries, and to retain their creative strength right up to the present time. Even more remarkable were the Diggers, or True Levellers, who established the clear outlines of democratic socialism, including a demand for the common ownership of land, for equal rights for women, for an accountable Parliament and for the provision of public services in health and education. All this was evolved two centuries before Marx illuminated the nature of capitalism and analysed the conflicts it would release.

All this is part of our rich inheritance, and it is there to be studied. In recent years this has come to light as a result of the work of men like H.N. Brailsford and Christopher Hill, whose books have revealed the real nature of the debates that took place during the English Civil War. Now Fenner Brockway has gathered the story together and recounted it for the general reader who might never have the opportunity to go back to the original pamphlets or records, or read the full history. The account given by Fenner Brockway is intensely readable and makes the events of that time seem to live as if they were part of the contemporary scene.

Almost all the issues which now form part of the present debate in Britain today came up for intense discussion at that time, and it is both interesting and deeply encouraging to know that the democratic and socialist traditions are so deeply rooted in our own national experience. But more than that, the future too will be shaped by what was said by our forefathers in that many of our own values derived from them. It is easy to identify a whole range of policies, and policy choices, that will have to be settled in the next few years which will be easier to make if we can understand what the Levellers and the Diggers were arguing about.

The political message left by the Levellers, the Agitators and the Diggers for today can easily be summarized and made relevant.

They would certainly be urging a redistribution of wealth and power in favour of working people and their families. They would be campaigning against the military-industrial complex with its world-wide network of influence. And there is no doubt about the attitude they would adopt towards the need for industrial democracy and the growth of trade unionism.

I believe that they would also look with the greatest of suspicion at the growing strength of the mass media which have taken over many of the characteristics of the medieval church in hunting down those who took up minority positions. The Levellers would demand the accountability of all power – civil, political, technical, educational and bureaucratic.

The modern movements towards a more responsible attitude towards the environment, together with a commitment to the common ownership of the land, to be held in trust for future generations, can all be traced back to the influence of the Diggers.

Above all, these seventeenth-century campaigns were for democracy and against the abuse of power, be it by the King or even a Lord Protector. For those who are still engaged in campaigns for these very principles, it is an immense comfort and source of strength to know that they have all been fought over before and that, as a result, the British people have got – albeit in their unconscious minds – some collective memories of what it is all about. That is what should give us the self-confidence to tackle the same forces today who represent the *status quo* and resist the march towards democracy. However long it takes, we know that these ideas of human freedom are undefeatable. Fenner Brockway's own life and work within the Labour Movement is a living proof of the fact.

1979   Tony Benn

Introduction

There have been many books about the Levellers, Agitators and Diggers. Why another? First because, while distinguished historians have written of every aspect of their activities and made available the original documents, there remains a need for a concise and straightforward description of the drama of the expanding revolution from its modest beginning in claiming religious toleration to the final defiance by the seizure of the common lands to establish socialist communities. Secondly, because of the necessity to bring home to all interested in social evolution, and particularly to present-day socialists, the significance of the seventeenth-century revolutionaries as the initiators of democratic socialist principles. This was particularly true of the Diggers, whose record, gathered from many sources, is perhaps told here more fully than before.

I have based my story of the Levellers almost entirely on the monumental work of H.N. Brailsford, *The Levellers in the English Revolution*, often using his own phrases, and I am grateful to his widow, Evamaria Brailsford, for permitting me to do so. Tragically, he died before he finished his work, and my chapter on the Diggers owes nearly everything to three other great books, D.W. Petergorsky's *Left Wing Democracy in the English Civil War*, G.H. Sabine's *The Works of Gerrard Winstanley*, and Christopher Hill's *Gerrard Winstanley, Law of Freedom and Other Writings*, though I have been able to add some items from personal research. In my final section, 'Conclusions', I have sought to relate the contributions of the Levellers, Agitators and Diggers, each separately, to the fundamental principles of modern democratic socialism.

Historians have been fortunate in documentation. Leveller petitions to the Commons are on record, and their many pamphlets preserved. Astonishingly full records of army gatherings in which the Agitators participated were made by secretary Clarke, including the historic proceedings of the army parliament at Putney Church, and in the works of Winstanley, the inspiration of the Diggers. The *Clarke Papers* were comprehensively edited by C.H. Firth in the 1890s, the basis of all we know. Strangely, their importance was first realized in Germany. Edward Bernstein, the socialist historian, published in 1895 *Cromwell and Communism, Socialism and Democracy*, and the Marxist theoretician, Karl Kautsky, referred to the role of both the Levellers and the Diggers. The great historian G.P. Gooch was the first writer in England to popularize Clarke's references to Winstanley in his *History of English Democratic Ideas in the Seventeenth Century* (1898), succeeded by G.M. Trevelyan's *England in the Seventeenth Century* (1904).

America followed, though not until 1916, when T.C. Pease wrote *The Leveller Movement*, giving rise to a series of works by followers of Henry George, excited by the Diggers, and by G.H. Sabine's massive work on Winstanley. Russia did not discover the Diggers to any great extent until 1967, when Professor Barg published in Moscow *Lower-Class Democracy in the English Bourgeois Revolution*, a typical Soviet title.

In 1947, we had M.A. Gibbs's *Life of John Lilburne*, and probably most of us have forgotten that the following year George Orwell and Reginald Reynolds edited *British*

Pamphleteers, emphasizing in this collection the communal pioneering of the Diggers. In 1955 – America again – Joseph Frank published his authoritative work *The Levellers*, Lilburne, Overton and Walwyn. Then, in 1961, came Brailsford's monumental work, edited posthumously and sympathetically by Christopher Hill, and also Pauline Gregg's newly informative *Life of John Lilburne*. Recently there has been a spate of books, including Howard Shaw's *The Levellers* (1968), Christopher Hill's captivating *The World Turned Upside Down* (1972), and Professor Aylmer's scholarly contribution to the *Documents of Revolution* series, *The Levellers in the English Revolution* (1975), with its splendid selection of illustrations. Finally, among more works too many to list, mention must be made of David Caute's brilliant novel, *Comrade Jacob*, which brings human warmth to the heroism and tragedy of the Diggers' camp at St George's Hill.

It will be seen that there is a wealth of treatment, but it also has to be said that the English Civil War period stays constantly open to the reassessments of historians, and that new information is constantly coming to light. We have to realize that, in dealing with the politics of radical groups in the 1640s, we are often dealing with the politics of the inarticulate and sometimes dependent on the evidence of hostile and hence biased witnesses. Thus there are difficulties in recovering the facts from among the dark patches in our knowledge of the past, but this remains a rich field for investigation, the period in English history when the principle of freedom of conscience for all men first truly asserted itself. My hope is that I have contributed a little to the debate in a new way.

1979   Fenner Brockway

Chronology of Main Events

1629 Charles I dissolves parliament and initiates period of 'personal rule'

1638 John Lilburne whipped and pilloried after his trial in Star Chamber for his part in smuggling proscribed pamphlets

1640 April   King forced to recall parliament to raise an army to suppress the rebellion in Scotland, prompted by attempts to introduce new Prayer Book there

May 5   Short Parliament dissolved

November 3   King forced to call new parliament after defeat of English army by Scots

Long Parliament proceeds to dismantle the Crown's prerogative power

1641 November   Rebellion breaks out in Ireland. The need to raise an army to suppress it forces the Commons to adopt more radical demands

1642 January   King withdraws from London after abortive attempt to arrest the leaders of the parliamentary opposition

August   Civil war begins with raising of King's standard at Nottingham

1645   New Model Army formed. Parliament wins battles of Naseby and Langport

1646   King surrenders to Scots; subsequently handed to Parliament

July 7   Publication of 'A remonstrance of many thousand citizens', commonly taken to date the entry into history of the Leveller 'party'

July 19   Lilburne imprisoned by Commons

1647   March   Presbyterian-dominated parliament, alarmed by growing radicalism and anxious to secure treaty with King, moves to disband army

April   Army mutinies. Election of agitators by the ranks

May   Army leadership joins with agitators in opposing parliament

June 4   King captured by Cornet Joyce and brought to the army

June 5   Army adopts *Solemn Engagement* at general rendezvous on Newmarket Heath

June 14   *Representation of the Army* asserts Army's right to an independent political voice; calls for an end to the present parliament and for a wider franchise in future elections

June 16   Army impeaches 11 most prominent members parliament

June 22   Commons invaded by London 'mob'. Presbyterian majority vote to invite King back to London

August   Army leadership offers 'Heads of Proposals' as basis for settlement with King and marches on London

October   Election of new agitators who present 'The case of the Army truly stated' for the Army Council to consider

October 28 – November 11   Putney Debates. *Agreement of the People* laid before the Army Council

November 11   Flight of King to the Isle of Wight

November 15   Mutiny in Army at rendezvous at Corkbush Field, Ware, in support of the *Agreement of the People* suppressed

1648   January   Leveller leaders Lilburne and Wildman arrested by Commons after addressing Leveller rally at Wapping

April   Second Civil War

September 11   Levellers' 'Large Petition' presented to Commons

October 29   Colonel Rainsborough, leading Leveller spokesman, murdered by royalists in the North

November   Failure of renewed negotiations between Levellers and Army leadership at Windsor

December 2   Army re-enters London

December 6   Pride's Purge of those hostile to Army in parliament

December 10   Second version of the *Agreement of the People* published by Levellers. Digger tract, *Light Shining in Buckinghamshire*, published

1649   January 30   Charles I executed

March   Monarchy and the House of Lords abolished Lilburne and other Leveller leaders arrested after publication of *Englands New Chains Discovered* attacking new régime

More Light Shining in Buckinghamshire published

April 1   Establishment of Diggers' colony at St George's Hill, near Walton-on-Thames

April 26   *The True Levellers Standard Advanced* published

May 1   Third version of the *Agreement of the People* published

Election of new agitators. Leveller-inspired mutiny in Army suppressed at Burford

Commonwealth proclaimed

September 21   Leveller petition, The Remonstrance of Many Thousands of the Free People of England, attracted 98,064 signatures

October 24   John Lilburne tried for treason and found not guilty by jury

November 8   Leveller leaders released from imprisonment

Diggers' colony at Cobham, Surrey (to which they had moved from St George's Hill) attacked by local gentry and freeholders

1650   April   Diggers finally forced to leave Cobham Heath

June 30   John Lilburne exiled by Rump Parliament

1652   *The Law of Freedom in a Platform*, Winstanley's final statement of Digger aims, published

1653   April   Rump expelled by Cromwell

July   Lilburne placed on trial after return from exile; found not guilty but imprisoned in the Tower before being transferred to Jersey

July 9   *The Fundamentall Laws and Liberties of England claimed . . . by severall peaceable persons . . . commonly called Levellers* published

December   After the failure of Barebone's Parliament, Cromwell appointed Lord Protector. Signals end of radical revolution by speech to first parliament attacking 'men of Levelling principles'

1656   May   Lilburne announces acceptance of Quaker faith

1657   August   Death of Lilburne

1660   Charles II restored

Preamble:
The Levellers, 1638–47

We have recently been rediscovering the Levellers and the Diggers. Michael Foot and Tony Benn, who somehow find time from their parliamentary duties for historical research, have said that they were our socialist ancestors. I add to their number the Agitators. Who were these Levellers, Agitators and Diggers?

For my generation, our school history books recording the English Revolution of the seventeenth century did not mention them. If we heard of them at all we were left with the impression that they were dissident groups of Utopians with no influence on events. This was emphatically not so of the Levellers and Agitators, who were the driving force for democracy, both among civilians and in the army. The Diggers, seeking to supplement political democracy by economic equality, were admittedly small communities, but their philosophy and practice extraordinarily expressed the principles and values of socialism. We have been slow to appreciate the significance of these revolutionaries. As I have indicated in my introduction, their influence has been recognized, since the research of the nineteenth century, in many authoritative books by distinguished authors. We have no reason to be ignorant.

An important element in our one British revolution was the contest it involved between authoritarianism and democracy, with the proviso that these terms at this stage of our political history involved instinctive more than intellectual thinking. The First Civil War occurred, at least in part, because Charles I claimed to be able to make laws and levy taxes irrespective of Parliament. Then religion came to be another element. Despite Britain's breach with Rome, Charles attempted to impose on the Presbyterians (who had become the State Church following the Elizabethan Settlement of 1559) ritual ceremonies which the Puritan-minded would not accept. Charles was disciplined, but he again challenged both democracy and conscience by attempting to arrest the five leading dissenters in Parliament and thrusting bishops on the Presbyterians in Scotland. So arose the First Civil War.

One is astonished now to realize the hold which religion had in those days. Reading the proceedings of the Long Parliament and about the activities of the Cromwellians, we find nearly every pronouncement made in the name of God. The pulpit had more influence than our modern media and was the major source of information and opinion. Whoever ruled the Church ruled the State. Perhaps it was therefore natural that, following the first defeat of Charles, the issue of freedom of conscience should become the test of democracy. The Presbyterians who dominated Parliament proved as authoritarian in the sphere of religion as the monarch had been. They made attendances at their services compulsory, and denied the rights not only of Catholics and Jews, but of fellow Puritans – Congregationalists and those groups which later coalesced into Baptists and Quakers – to meet or preach. The Levellers came into being to claim tolerance.

In their origins, the Levellers were 'middle of the road', as they described themselves, representative of the tradesmen, the craftsmen, the journeymen, the weavers, printers, brass founders and other skilled guildsmen. The top classes were the landowners and the merchants, more particularly the aristocratic families with great estates and those who controlled the Merchant Adventurers Company and the East India Company, which had a monopoly of foreign trade, and the Stationers' Company, which had a monopoly of publication and printing. In social terms, there were two confrontations: the urban producers against the merchants and small farmers and copyholders against the great landowners. At first the Levellers were participants in the former only; later, as we shall see, they identified themselves to some extent with the small farmers. For some time, the Levellers' demands were political – they wanted democracy to protect their status and livelihood – but as the struggle developed, so their programme extended to economic and social claims for equality.

The four leaders were Richard Overton, William Walwyn, John Wildman and John Lilburne. Overton had been a Baptist refugee in the more liberal Holland when a boy, became a printer in London and served the Leveller cause by clandestinely publishing its pamphlets. He was well educated, spoke and wrote well, reasoning calmly without the emotional religious obsession so persistent generally. Walwyn had an establishment upbringing – son of a Worcestershire squire and the grandson of a bishop, he actually became a member of the Merchant Adventurers Company after his apprenticeship in London. Because of his status, the religious and social élite hated him most among the Levellers. Perhaps this was also because of his cleverness and cunning in presenting the case for the cause he espoused. Wildman, who emerged a little after the others, was more the political legalist, whose logical mind had an important value, though he contributed little that was original in Leveller thought.

John Lilburne, on the other hand, was the truly dynamic figure, cruder and fiercer in speech and writing than his colleagues, but of spectacular courage and popular appeal. He was instinctively a rebel, defying authority without thought of personal consequences. The extraordinary feature of his campaign was that it was conducted mostly from prison, where he continued to write pamphlets, maintain contact with activists outside, plan their action, and even penetrate the army so that the ranks became partners with the Levellers. But all this lies ahead.

John's father was a distressed landowner, too poor to set up his son as a weaver after he had finished his apprenticeship. John therefore suffered the privations of unemployment, but soon became involved in political activity. He was bitterly opposed to episcopacy, and he readily joined in a plot to have printed in Holland and smuggled back to England a pamphlet written by Dr Bastwick, a Puritan merchant (later a renegade), denouncing efforts by Charles I to reimpose Catholic practices on the Presbyterian State Church. John was given away by an accomplice, arrested, and arraigned before the Star Chamber and the Lord Privy Seal.

The trial made Lilburne a popular hero. The court was stunned when this stripling of about twenty-three challenged its jurisdiction. He refused to pay the clerk's fee, to take the oath or answer incriminating questions. That anyone should defy the exalted Star Chamber and the highest judge in the land was incredible, and the punishment was severe. He was sentenced to three years' imprisonment, stripped to the waist, dragged at a cart's tail and flogged the whole way from Fleet prison, through the Strand and Whitehall, to Westminster. There he was put in a pillory. His head clamped, he made a passionate speech to the large crowd which had gathered, defending Dr Bastwick, ending by throwing two or three hidden copies of his pamphlet to outstretched hands. He was thereupon gagged and returned to prison.

For some months in prison, Lilburne was shackled with heavy irons on both wrists and ankles and became weak with fever and semi-starvation. The common prison in the seventeenth century stank with excrement and was alive with vermin. He became so ill that he was moved to better quarters, where to his relief, he could receive food and visitors. He exploited the limited opportunities to engage in continued campaigning. He began to write pamphlets, smuggled out by a maidservant, protesting against his treatment, and Overton and Walwyn had some of them printed by their underground press, while a growing band of supporters distributed them widely.

Anger rose and there were riots, public indignation becoming so strong that Lilburne was permitted to petition Parliament. It is noteworthy that Cromwell's first speech in the Commons was an appeal for the release of Lilburne, and it was so powerful that a motion was carried condemning his imprisonment as 'illegal, bloody, wicked, cruel, barbarous and tyrannical', and recognizing his right to reparation. Lilburne was reprieved though not released immediately, and Cromwell became his idol.

There will be many references to petitions to Parliament. In the seventeenth century and long afterwards the House of Commons was required to take the consideration of petitions as the first business of any sitting — very different from today when they disappear in a green bag and are not heard of again. The Levellers exploited this privilege with great effect throughout their history.

When civil war broke in 1642, Lilburne enlisted as a captain, was taken prisoner, threatened with execution. He was saved by his wife, Elizabeth, who was no less courageous and forthright in action than John. She rushed violently into the Commons, addressed the astonished Members from the bar, and won from them a threat of retaliation should the King authorize execution. Although heavy with child, she then hastened to Oxford, where the royal headquarters were stationed, plunged through the guards, and faced the King's counsellors. With the parliamentary motion in her hand, she warned that retaliatory executions would involve prominent Royalists and urged that an exchange of prisoners would be of mutual benefit. Astonishingly, she succeeded — an instance of bold initiative which deserves a place in the roll of heroic revolutionary women.

In London, Lilburne was acclaimed by cheering crowds. Rejoining the army, he was made a major by Cromwell and his own bravery and skill in action brought him the rank of lieutenant-colonel. Then came an issue of conscience to which he responded characteristically. He was offered a higher command, but this required taking the Covenant oath which implied the suppression by force of minority religious communities. In accordance with the principle of freedom of conscience to which he adhered, Lilburne could not accept this and, much to the regret of Cromwell, he resigned from the army. Lilburne was one of Cromwell's favourites. They were even bedfellows on the march, 'talking over everything and everybody'.

Back in civilian life, Lilburne renewed his agitation more strongly than ever. In eagerly distributed pamphlets, he attacked the Presbyterian-ruled Parliament (Puritan but authoritarian) so vigorously for its absence of toleration that he was arraigned a second time with a string of devastating consequences. First, on 19 July 1645, he was summoned before a committee of the House of Commons to answer charges of having spread scandal concerning certain Members of Parliament. He protested against the committee's right to try him, refused to answer questions and was promptly sent to Newgate for three months. Nine months later, on 11 July 1646, the House of Lords called on him to answer charges of having defamed the Earl of Manchester in his unlicensed pamphlets. The earl himself chaired the hearing, but Lilburne again took a stand over the question of its jurisdiction, claiming that the Lords had no rights to try a commoner. He was the first man in history to make such an audacious claim, but the Lords packed him off once more to Newgate before summoning him back to hear the results of their deliberations. At the bar of the House, Lilburne declined to kneel, remained covered and stopped his ears with his hands while the charge was read. He then made a spirited attack on his judges, and for his reward was fined £2,000 (a fortune in those days), denied the right to hold any office, civil or military, and sentenced to seven years' imprisonment, while his pamphlets were burned by the common hangman. From Lilburne's earlier imprisonment, the motivation of the Levellers had arisen. This second savage sentence incited organized action. Overton and Walwyn got busy, with the result that over 2,000 citizens of London signed a petition to Parliament, while hundreds of women, recruited by Elizabeth, lobbied the Members. Overton wrote a pamphlet defending Lilburne, which led to his arrest also, and he and his wife and brother suffered brutal violence similar to that meted out to his leader: they were dragged through the streets to Newgate. London was afire as a consequence, and tens of thousands marched in protest.

Even before Lilburne was under trial by the Lords, Overton and Walwyn, probably with the help of Henry Marten, radical republican, and never-failing champion of liberty, in the Commons had been writing the *Remonstrance*, a manifesto addressed to Parliament which became the basic declaration of the Levellers in their first stage, though the name was not used for a year yet. Published in July 1646, four days before Lilburne's first hearing before the Upper House, it called for the abolition of the Lords, demanded the dissolution of Parliament, proclaimed the sovereignty of the people, insisted on equality before the law and the ending of imprisonment for debt, advocated the destruction of the monopoly of foreign trade by the Merchant Adventurers Company (later the East India Company and the Stationers' Company were added), the only economic demand and, with emphasis, asserted freedom of conscience and the toleration of all religions. The spirit of the manifesto is expressed in this paragraph:

> Ye are rich and abound in goods, and have need of nothing; but the afflictions of the poor, your hunger-starved brethren, ye have no compassion of... you suffer poor Christians, for whom Christ died, to kneel before you in the streets, aged, sick and crippled, begging your half-penny

charities, and ye rustle by them in your coaches and silks daily without regard or taking any course for their constant relief. Their sight would melt the heart of any Christian, and yet it moves not you nor your clergy.

Lilburne made his foetid prison an office for organization and propaganda. He instigated his London supporters to force their way into the Guildhall to claim the right of the citizens to elect the City Mayor. They were violently prevented from entering, but Lilburne used the controversy which followed to popularize his pamphlet *London's Liberty in Chains*, in which he denounced the administration of the City and the composition of Parliament as travesties of true democracy. He had reason. The City was dominated by the merchant monopolists and Parliament by the landowning gentry – the Upper House by the great landowners, the Commons by their sons and dependants, the squirearchy and a few merchants and lawyers.

Lilburne's disillusion with the Long Parliament was so great that he warned his readers that, unless they changed its membership, they would gain nothing from the civil war but a 'change of masters'. Milton had said the same thing: 'The new Presbyter is but the old Priest writ larger.' There was the scandal of the 'rotten boroughs', which could be bought for £40 and often had only three electors. Lilburne was the first to make this issue a living controversy, though it was a long time before their abolition was achieved. Cromwell, when he became Protector, did abolish the 'decayed' constituencies, but he reversed his decision in later authoritarian days. It was nearly two hundred years before Lilburne's initiative was fulfilled.

Lilburne's pamphlet indicated further developments of the thinking of the Levellers. For the first time there was a commitment to manhood suffrage – a little surprisingly *not* for women, since Baptists and the dissident section of the Congregationalists recognized sex equality when electing their ministers (though, illogically, they had to be men). Philosophically, Lilburne himself did so. 'Every particular and individual man and woman that ever breathed in the world,' he wrote, 'are and were by nature all equal and alike in power, dignity, authority and majesty, none of them having any authority, dominion or magisterial power one over... another.' Not all men were to be enfranchised by the Leveller proposal. Personal servants and beggars were to be excluded, the former on the ground that they would be intimidated by their masters. Even so, the principle of manhood suffrage was a revolutionary idea three centuries ago.

A second petition to Parliament indicated further advances in policy. The first of these was opposition to the death penalty for petty thefts (though the Levellers were the first to demand the execution of Charles I). The second new inclusion was significant. Perhaps it was a deputation to Parliament of 2,000 farmers and copyholders in protest against tithes which led Lilburne, Walwyn and Overton to realize that this group could become formidable recruits to their movement. In their petition, the demand was made 'that tithes and all other enforced maintenance may be for ever abolished and nothing in place thereof imposed'. Tithes were an intolerable burden on both large and small farmers. One tenth of their income was confiscated to maintain the Presbyterian clergy, an appreciable proportion also going straight into the pockets of the gentry. When too poor to pay, their cattle, pigs or chickens were commandeered. Baptists and radicals among the Congregationalists refused payment, while Quakers sold their farms to become traders rather than do so. It was the exploited copyholders, however, whom the Levellers had most in mind; many of them were imprisoned when they could not pay the tithes. The 9,000 Presbyterian clergy were unintentionally the best propagandists for the Levellers. In parishes throughout England, the pulpit was used to denounce them as 'enemies of God' for opposing tithes, and the tenant farmers turned to Lilburne and his associates as influential champions. From this moment the Levellers added 'and peasants' to their self-description as 'middle of the road'. Characteristically, the Parliament of landowners ordered

31

their petition to be burned by the common hangman, for the Levellers' radical challenge over tithes was a direct attack on their incomes.

Part One:
The Agitators, 1646–8

Meanwhile, a revolt parallel to that of the Levellers was developing in the army. The New Model Army, which was gathered together to fight Charles in the First Civil War, was composed of a mixture of dedicated volunteers and pressed men, the conscripts being in a slight majority. The Presbyterian leader, Denzil Holles, described most of its colonels and officers as 'mean tradesmen, brewers, tailors, goldsmiths, shoemakers and the like, a notable dunghill', a biased but partially true view. The New Model should really be defined as a volunteer army, some of whose officers were promoted from below the social level of the gentry. The ranks probably contained a large urban presence along with the peasantry. Once Charles had been defeated, the New Model Army was kept enrolled because of the threat from Scotland and the rebellion in Ireland. The problem then arose of meeting the cost — and it is noteworthy that the Levellers, again historic pioneers, urged that the money should be raised by direct taxation proportionate to income.

Officers and men were seriously in arrears of payment, and they presented a petition to Parliament demanding a settlement, including allowances for widows, orphans and disabled, and payment for their quarters. Supplementing these monetary claims was a significant protest against pressure to serve in Ireland. Parliament was outraged that, to quote Holles, the army should 'make their will a rule that all the interests of King, Parliament, and Kingdom must be ignored by', and it summoned to the bar three senior officers who were said to have promoted the petition, among them Colonel Robert Lilburne, brother and colleague of John. They were rebuked, instructed to suppress the petition, and all who advanced it were denounced as 'enemies of the State', a charge remembered.

The top generals, including Cromwell, concurred in this condemnation, but anger in the army was great, and junior officers and men of sixteen regiments, assisted by the advice of the Levellers, took the unprecedented step of forming a soldiers' council with two elected representatives from each. These representatives became historically known as 'Agitators', though in fact they were no more than agents for their regiments. Perhaps the term was a popular rendering of 'adjudicators', perhaps it was attached to them because of their later militancy. One of the first demands of the soldiers' council was that officers should be elected by the ranks.

This radicalism undoubtedly reflected the temper of the troops. They were not the normal regimented army but groups of spirited men, spontaneous volunteers against a dictatorial monarch but equally resistant to dictatorship by the class-élitist Parliament. A large proportion of them were Baptists and dissenting Congregationalists, the most committed of the Puritans, resenting also the intolerance of the Presbyterians, who as the Established Church arrogantly denied the rights of other denominations. There is no doubt that the Levellers played a large part in influencing and even organizing the militants in the army. A trooper, Edward Sexby, acted as a go-between. He was a born conspirator, led a fantastically adventurous life, ending it in prison for advocating the assassination of Cromwell. For the moment, however, his plotting was limited to Leveller aspirations. Lilburne claimed that he himself had the main responsibility for the troops' revolt; perhaps this was egotistic, but the propaganda in his pamphlets and the advice which he continually sent out from prison certainly affected army thinking and action. Overton had equal influence. At first, outside prison, he was able to be constantly at the service of the Agitators, and his mature counsel was generally followed. In addition, many of the leaders of army action, including Rainsborough, who was a colonel, were themselves among the Levellers.

It became clear to Parliament that the New Model Army would have to be disbanded if it were not to become a revolutionary instrument, and a plan was prepared to place the forces under reliable Presbyterian control. As a first step, the non-Presbyterian generals, including Cromwell and his colleague and son-in-law, Ireton, were to be dismissed. It was soon evident that the New Model Army would resist the change. The Agitators drafted a letter and took it to the bar of the Commons. They demanded a withdrawal of the condemnation that they and their fellows were 'enemies of the State', attacked the proposal that the army should be broken 'in pieces', once again called for the payment of their arrears of pay and for security for widows, orphans and the disabled, and stated bluntly that they would not volunteer for service in Ireland 'until our just desires be granted'.

No doubt these more self-interested demands were most prominent in the minds of the troops, but the influence of the Levellers was evident when the authors of the statement added that their 'liberties as Englishmen are 10,000 times more important than our pay arrears'. Parliament responded by appointing a commission of investigation whose members, to win confidence, included Cromwell and Ireton. Its recommendations deepened the anger of the army. Arrears among the troopers mounted to fifty-two weeks, and the commission proposed only that an earlier promise to pay off six weeks should be extended to a mere eight weeks. At this moment Cromwell, for associating himself with these recommendations, lost much of the trust of the junior officers and men and the disillusionment was increased when he said in the Commons that the army would accept disbandment and exhorted its officers to promote obedience to Parliament.

The Agitators, who, it should be remembered, were the elected spokesmen of each regiment (direct ancestors of the shop stewards in factories today), replied defiantly. 'We have been quiet and peaceable in obeying all orders and commands,' they wrote, 'yet we now have a just cause to tell you; if we be not relieved in these our grievances we shall be forced to that which we pray God to direct.' It was the first hint of rebellion. The Agitators then addressed their appeal to the public, and the Levellers gave them the facilities of their printing press at Oxford for the wide distribution of re-peated petitions to Parliament. An important development was cooperation between the army and peasantry. The sol-diers were quartered in the private houses of villagers and won their sympathy by demanding that Parliament should meet the indebtedness due to them. Instigated by the Levellers, the peasants, particularly in East Anglia, poured out a flood of petitions in favour of the army, adding an expression of their own grievances, particularly the scandal of their impoverish-ment by tithe confiscations in contrast with the corruptions practised by Members of Parliament and the sordid purchase of the 'rotten boroughs'.

The crisis in the conflict between the army and Parliament developed in a rapid series of events. Cromwell recovered credibility by getting a parliamentary majority to make many concessions, including an audit of the men's accounts of arrears, security on leaving the services for any remaining ar-rears, provision for widows, orphans, and the disabled, and a promise of no pressure in recruiting an army for Ireland. General Fairfax, the commander, took advantage of these concessions to impose discipline. Assuring the regiments that their grievances would be redressed, he forbade any further activity by the Agitators and prohibited meetings of the troops or any consultation with them. It looked as though Parliament had won the day.

But the Agitators took no notice of their commander's prohibitions. In a strongly worded letter to General Fairfax, they asked him to call the whole army to a rendezvous so that its opinion could be taken, repeating resistance to disbandment until grievances had actually been redressed, and sounding the warning that the men would, if necessary, act with or without the support of the officers. Instead of a rendezvous, Fairfax called a meeting of the Army Council, but found to his dismay that by eighty votes to five it endorsed the Agitators' line. Action followed – regiment after regiment drove out their few Presbyterian officers. Parliament reacted by sending a commission to make arrangements for the disbanding of the offending regiments – the Agitators scoffed, 'they may as well send them among so many bears to take away their whelps'. The troops were ordered to surrender at Chelmsford. Instead, they marched to Newmarket to hold the army rendezvous. Parliament gave way. The commission was recalled.

There followed an event full of national high drama. *The Agitators took King Charles prisoner!* The King was under parliamentary detention at Oxford. When 500 men under a very junior young officer, Cornet George Joyce, arrived at Holmby House, where the monarch was held, the guard embraced them as comrades and the King had no option except to receive them and even accompany them. 'Tell me what commission you have?' he asked Cornet Joyce. 'Here is my commission,' the young subaltern replied. 'Where?' said the King. 'Behind me,' Joyce answered, pointing to his troops. The King concurred. He was confined at Woburn Abbey.

In the meantime Parliament was recruiting forces and storing ammunition independently of the army. The Agitators probably feared that unilateral moves would be made to free and restore the King. Very probably their fear was supplemented by acceptance of a heavily backed rumour that the mistrusted Denzil Holles, the Queen and the Scots

were conspiring to remove the King from Holmby House to renew the civil war. The view that the Agitators believed in such a
possibility is supported by extraordinary action taken by the
Leveller colonel, Thomas Rainsborough, simultaneously with
the abduction of the King. He was under orders to lead a force
to Jersey; instead, he gave way to, probably encouraged, a
mutiny of his men, who proceeded to Oxford where they took
possession of Parliament's large store of ammunition and their
artillery train. The New Model Army now had under its own
control the means to meet any forces which might seek to restore the King on terms other than its own, which, it was determined, must be compatible with toleration and democracy.

There was another surprise. Cromwell, who had comprom-
ised in Parliament, came out openly on the side of the army.
He rode from London to join the insurgent troops at their
rendezvous. We know he had secretly seen Cornet Joyce
before his capture of King Charles at Oxford. Did Cromwell
believe the rumour of the Royalist conspiracy? Whatever the
reason, his action began to reveal his true nature, seeking
influence where power was.

Cromwell's identification with the army and their spokesmen the Agitators had a decisive effect. Parliament retreated
still further. By ninety-six votes to seventy-nine the Members
decided to withdraw the slur that the army were 'enemies of
the State'. Arrears in payment were to be paid fully, subject to
deduction for free quarters. At their rendezvous the troops
acclaimed their victory but were not appeased. Parliament
was still set on disbandment and was encouraging Presbyterian officers to serve in a reconstituted politically reliable
force. When a new commission was sent to press for acceptance of Parliament's terms, and General Fairfax again urged
concurrence, the rendezvous with a great cry of unanimity
decided instead to refer the decision to its representative
council. The result was less than the Agitators desired.
Cromwell was still a moderating influence, and he got the
council to appoint Ireton to draft the army's statement.

Representation of the Army, while repeating the army's opposition to disbandment until grievances were redressed, was mostly a political manifesto reflecting many of Cromwell's unacceptable views. While it urged that Parliament should be purged of its more reactionary members, it proposed that membership should be composed of the 'morally righteous and the religious', a saintly élite, which the Levellers opposed as undemocratic. It accorded with Levellers' demands by calling for the dissolution of Parliament (the Long Parliament persisted for eight years), fixed periods between elections, and the abolition of the 'rotten boroughs', but it shocked them by accepting the restoration of the King under conditions consistent with 'the freedom of the subject', and it actually acknowledged Presbyterianism as the Established Church with its tithes and discipline; a plea for freedom of conscience was timidly worded. Compromise had won.

Meanwhile, the City came to the rescue of Parliament. Its Lord Mayor and council presented a petition for the liberation of the King from the army so that free access to him could be assured and asking for power to raise a force of cavalry to defend Church and kingdom. Gratefully the Commons consented. The army reacted with vigour. With Cromwell at their head, the troops moved towards London and sent an ultimatum to the City saying that they were 'drawing near your city', but no one need suffer if assistance were not given to 'that wicked party that would embroil us and the kingdom'. If, however, 'you be seduced to take up arms in opposition to our just undertakings', the army would wash its hands of the ruin that would follow. Parliament rallied to the City, setting up a Committee of Supply to raise horse and foot to cooperate with its militia. When, undeterred, the army marched to St Albans, the Lord Mayor summoned every man to join the City's forces on pain of death.

It looked as though a civil war would be renewed, not between the people and the Royalists but between the people and the undemocratic Parliament. Then an extraordinary thing happened, showing the strength of following which the Levellers had in London. *There was massed refusal to join the City forces despite the threat of death* – some companies counted ten men, others none at all. The army had won without a shot. There was nothing for Parliament and the City to do except apologize, the latter promising not to raise forces. The City asked the army to stay twenty miles from London; Parliament ordered them to retire thirty miles; the army rested at St Albans, twenty miles.

For some months there was manoeuvring by Parliament, the City and the army, not only militarily but politically. It was a period of confusion, difficult to analyse and describe. When the army moved forward to Uxbridge, Parliament and City became subdued; when General Fairfax withdrew the troops to Bedford, the City became aggressive, re-establishing its own militia. The determining conflict, however, was political rather than military, controversy exploding between Parliament and the army, between both and the King, between the Agitators and compromising Cromwell, and between the Levellers and the Presbyterian establishment. All these issues were debated in the Council of the Army, unique in history as a democratic forum in the forces, in which privates and subalterns argued freely with the generals. At first there was unanimity between men and officers, though among the former the psychological climate of 'them and us' remained. They united in demands which included the release of Lilburne and 'the Overtons', now in prison.

Overton had written a moving appeal to Fairfax, 'and to all the officers and soldiers under his command'. He wrote amid the stench and vermin of Newgate, and yet achieved a notable alliance of reason and passion. He had reason for passion. His wife was held in Bridewell with 'bawds and strumpets'; his brother was in another prison; his children were scattered among neighbours. With brief dignity he wrote about these family sufferings, urging that the imprisonments were illegal, but the greater part of his appeal dealt with the wrongs of the people. He expressed the known political demands of the

Levellers, but added new social demands, a reflection of the advance of some Leveller thinking. Brailsford even writes that he aimed at the Welfare State by the provision of hospitals and accommodation for the aged, the sick, the infirm, and widows and orphans, all erected and maintained at the public expense, though in accordance with Leveller emphasis on participating democracy, he urged decentralization through local control. A bold demand for the ending of all enclosures of common land followed. Overton went on to make a forthright attack on Parliament for failing to act as the trustee of the rights and freedoms of the people, for its treatment of the army and its imprisonment of political opponents. He argued that the Long Parliament, composed of the economic élite, elected on a restrictive franchise and shamelessly maintaining itself in office, had no democratic authority, and even argued that armed revolt would be justified.

'Now is no time to sit thumbing caps [he wrote] . If they will not *give* us leave to use our tongues and our pens to present and make known our grievances, we must *take* leave to make use of our hands and swords for the defence and redemption of our lives, our laws and our liberties from the hand of the destroyer, for our safety must be maintained.'

He ended with an exhortation to the Agitators to preserve their strength, warning that if they were befooled of their power, then 'farewell our hopes in the Army, for I am confident that it must be the poor, the simple and mean things of this earth that must confound the mighty and the strong'. It is not surprising that this moving appeal led the Agitators to make their demand for the release of the Overtons as well as of Lilburne. A little generously, in view of Overton's last remarks, the officers joined them.

It is doubtful if the officers would have been so conciliatory if they had read already what Lilburne wrote immediately afterwards. It openly incited conflict between the ranks and the command.

'Every individual private soldier whether horse or foot,' he wrote, 'ought freely to have their vote, to choose the transaction of their affairs, or else, in the sight of God and all rational men, are discharged from obeying, stooping or submitting to what is done by them [the officers].' If the command usurped power to act without this consent, their conduct 'merits a kicking out of the army', if nothing worse. Lilburne frankly named Cromwell and his associates as the officers he had in mind. He asserted that Cromwell and 'the rest of [his] fellow great ones...have bought and sold the laws, liberties and justice of the Kingdom for [their] own ends and greatness', and accused the general of 'robbing by unjust subtlety and shifting tricks the honest and gallant Agitators of all their power and authority'.

That was, for the time being, at least, exaggerated, for the Agitators soon showed their power. Indeed, the influence of the Agitators never seemed greater than at this point. Their emissaries had just won over the eight regiments in the North, stationed to resist any incursion by the Scots, who not only elected Agitators to represent them on the Army Council, but who went to the extreme of deposing their general when he disagreed, conveying him, a prisoner, far south to Reading where at last Fairfax gained their consent for his release. The confident ranks in the army were not content with calling for the release of Lilburne and the Overtons. They demanded the exclusion from Parliament of Baron Holles, the most reactionary Presbyterian leader, and ten associates – known as the notorious 'Eleven Members' – the restoration of public control of the London militia, the unification of all the armed forces under Fairfax, and punctual payment of the troops. They proposed that the army should march at once to London or near it to demonstrate their power to the City.

The Agitators were not yet convinced of the apostasy of Cromwell and Ireton. At the Army Council the two generals agreed to the presentation of these demands to Parliament, but were against a march on London. Ireton wished that proposals which he had formulated, known as the Heads of the Proposals, should be adopted and published before the army took action. Cromwell took the hopeful view that Parliament would be responsive and urged that the army should seek an understanding with it. 'What we gain in a free way,' he said, 'it is better than twice so much in a forced.' In the end, after a modest appeal by Cromwell for unity − 'if you be in the right and I am in the wrong, if we be divided I doubt we shall all be in the wrong' − a compromise was reached. The Agitators' demands should be sent as an ultimatum to Parliament, but a march on London would be postponed until its answer was received. Meantime, a committee of officers, including the Leveller General Rainsborough, was appointed to consider the draft of Ireton's Heads of the Proposals. Events proved that Cromwell was right in his interpretation of the mind of Parliament, that the Agitators were right in their suspicions of the City.

The demands which the generals submitted to Parliament were, in fact, far less drastic than the Agitators had proposed. The call for the release of Lilburne and the Overtons was only added as a postscript and, instead of immediate liberation and reparation, the request was made for their speedy trial and release on bail. Parliament had the sense to judge where the generals were in earnest and where they were less so. Fairfax was made commander of all the forces, the 'Eleven Members' were given leave of absence, the old control of the militia was re-established, and the additional concession was made that any cooperation in bringing foreign forces, including Scots, into the country would be designated treason. But about Lilburne and the Overtons Parliament took no action whatsoever.

So satisfied were the generals with this response that they transferred the headquarters of the army from Reading to Bedford and dispersed the cavalry to places as distant as Bristol and Newark. Cromwell, whether from generosity (he soon forgot verbal injuries) or from appreciation of his influence, visited John Lilburne in prison. The general expressed fear that the Leveller, if free, would stir trouble in the army, to which Lilburne astonishingly replied that if the Commons would quash his sentence and pay him compensation, he would restart life overseas. Was this weakness or strategy?

Cromwell left with 'divers fair promises', but immediately let Lilburne down. When a committee chaired by Marten reported in John's favour, the general voted for the report to be recommitted.

In 1647 the committee appointed by the Army Council to consider Ireton's Heads of the Proposals produced its terms for peace. It was a precise and constructive document, but again there were compromises. It began by asking that the Long Parliament should be dissolved within a year and should meet biennially for eight months. During the lengthy vacations, government should be carried on by a Council of State and committees. Constituencies would be proportionate to tax returns (though not to the number of citizens, as proposed by the Levellers), thus abolishing the 'rotten boroughs'. The restoration of the King, however, was accepted on conditions less stringent than even the Presbyterians had proposed in Parliament. If he declined to sign a Bill passed by Parliament (or if the Lords rejected), it was proposed that, when the lower House repassed the measure in its next session, it should automatically become law – an extraordinary anticipation of Lloyd George's Parliament Act of 1911.

Parliament was given control of all the armed forces and 'would have its say' in choosing 'the great officers'. On the issue of religious tolerance, so dear to the Levellers, the decision was a little vague, but its implications were favourable. 'All coercive power, authority and jurisdiction' by ecclesiastical officers would be ended, which meant that the State Church could not prohibit active Episcopalians or dissident Puritans from freedom to worship. Practices in worship or oaths 'objectionable to scrupulous consciences' were to be swept away, but Catholics were rather obscurely disabled from 'disturbing the State'. A list of urgent reforms was added to the Proposals, among them the lifting of taxes on commodities necessary to the poor, the abolition of monopolies (such as the Merchant Adventurers), some remedy for tithes and imprisonment for debt, and an endorsement that no alleged offender could be compelled to incriminate himself. These recommendations embodied many of the Levellers' demands, reflecting the influence of the twelve Agitators on the committee.

Despite its compromises, if the Heads of the Proposals had been accepted, immediate history would have been transformed. There would have been no Rump Parliament, no Cromwell protectorate, no conflict before the restoration of the monarchy. There would have been a peace settlement.

But it was not to happen. The Presbyterians in Parliament would not accept the limitations of the status of their Church by the acceptance of religious tolerance. The King rejected the Proposals. When the document was handed to him at Woburn Abbey by a deputation from the New Model Army, he told the troops, 'You cannot do without me, you will fall to ruin if I do not sustain you.' Rainsborough, the Leveller general, was so outraged that he rode to Bedford and spread throughout the army a report of the King's arrogance. The troops' anger 'became white hot' when a report reached them that the King was intriguing with the Scots, and perhaps with the City, for a renewal of the war. The Agitators invaded the lodging of the Scots' envoy, the Earl of Lauderdale, who was negotiating the invasion, and drove him to London. Only later was he allowed to meet the King.

But the *counter*-revolution was on. With the approval of the City oligarchy, 100,000 men signed a solemn *Engagement* to bring back the King to London on his own terms, 'in honour, safely to freedom', to conclude a personal treaty with 'his two Houses of Parliament' (note the *his*) and 'that without the nearer approach of the army'. A City mob invaded the Lords and the Commons and extorted from them not only the restoration of the City committee to control the militia, but an invitation to the King to return to London. These decisions were made amid violence and, when a majority of members refused to adjourn at the command of the chair, two Speakers (both moderates), eight Peers and fifty-seven M.P.s withdrew to place themselves under the protection of the army. The Presbyterian remnant thereupon selected new Speakers,

47

welcomed back the 'Eleven Members', forbade the army to approach within thirty miles, named a Committee of Safety to defend London and in St James's Fields (as the park was then called) Major-General Massey reviewed the improvised forces.

The reaction of the troops, officers and men was immediate. They decided to march to London. The battle was joined. The army assigned to Rainsborough the conduct of the encircling movement. It proved incredibly easy. The Levellers of Southwark opened the gates of their borough to him, and no sooner had he pointed his guns at the defences of London Bridge than the resistance of the City collapsed. Westminster surrendered without a shot. Rainsborough's men, 18,000 strong, with laurels in their hats, marched through the City. The Agitators exultant, the Army Council, took charge.

Parliament capitulated. The Speakers and their followers resumed their seats while Holles's 'Eleven Members' fled to the Continent. But the Presbyterians still had a majority, and they plucked up courage to defeat motions from the moderates to declare 'null and void' the votes extracted by the City mob which had invaded Parliament. There was angry reaction in the army to this revival of City power. The Agitators addressed a petition to Commander Fairfax, calling for a sweeping purge of the sixty-five members who continued to sit in 'that pretended Parliament' when the two Speakers had declared the House adjourned. The Army Council endorsed this call, and Cromwell was prepared to lead the men in action. He was thwarted by Fairfax delaying military orders. Parliament's fear of the army nevertheless remained. When a few days later Fairfax posted a regiment of horse in Hyde Park, a Commons majority, under threat of being purged, hastened to carry the motion, declaring the City votes null and void, the rejection of which had so angered the troops.

The King, at this time was, in Brailsford's words, playing a double game. He was pretending to be conciliatory while really hoping for a Scottish invasion. He declared he was prepared to negotiate on the terms of the Heads of the Proposals and encouraged Cromwell and Ireton to be optimistic by avowing he would agree to religious tolerance. In fact, he was dissembling – a bishop had assured him that he would have the Church's blessing if under pressure he gave this assurance while intending to repudiate it when the opportunity arose. On the political and social demands of the army, the King prevaricated, appearing to concede, reverting to obstruction. After weeks of fruitless negotiation, the Agitators became impatient, blaming not only the King for his filibustering but the generals for their continued faith in him. There was another reason for loss of confidence, less rational but very human. Cromwell's family, particularly the women, began to attend the Court functions which Charles maintained even in captivity. This social appeasement in fact occasioned more disgust than the political appeasement. Whispering spread from privates in the army to moderates at Westminster who had previously been devotees of Cromwell. In the Army Council, the discussions became ill-tempered. During an altercation with Cromwell, Rainsborough exclaimed 'one of us must not live'.

This emotive diversion destroyed the unity of the anti-Presbyterians in Parliament. When Henry Marten moved that 'no further addresses' be permitted to the King, Cromwell as well as Ireton voted with the opposing majority of eighty-four against thirty-four. The King's delaying tactics and the bitter spirit within the army and Parliament killed any hope that the Heads of the Proposals would provide a bridge to peace. Cromwell delivered a three-hour speech in the Commons which left the rift with the Agitators and Levellers seemingly beyond repair. He defended the institution of monarchy, said that his aim in the civil war had been to strengthen and not destroy it, and pleaded with the Commons to re-establish the Throne without delay.

Frustrated, the revolutionaries in the army and the Levellers adopted a new tactic. They decided no longer to co-operate with generals or Parliament, and to unite soldiers and people in a new form of government from below which would supersede the establishment. It is a little difficult to convey the conception behind this unprecedented proposal. In effect, the suggestion was that a democratic alliance of army and civilians, representing the sovereign people, should limit the powers of Parliament as well as those of the monarch – there should be a charter of human rights binding on Parliament guaranteeing personal liberties, freedom of religion, freedom from pressganged conscription and equality before the law. These three 'native rights' were stated in a notable document, *The Agreement of the People*, addressed to the Council of the Army by a reconstituted body of Agitators, representing sixteen regiments. The declaration was almost legally precise – commentators have asked whether Walwyn was the author. It was moderate, seeking a permanent peace. It included a conciliatory clause requiring a complete indemnity and amnesty for those engaged on both sides in the civil war. How was *The Agreement* to be adopted? Parliament could not be asked to enact it because it claimed an authority superior to Parliament, the direct power of the people. The first need was to get endorsement from the Army Council. After that it was proposed that a national convention should be called to frame a final text for submission to the people at large.

The historic meeting of the General Council of the Army was held in Putney Church from 28 October to 11 November, 1647, a gathering of privates, officers and generals in which all were equals, a parliament of the whole army. It assembled in an atmosphere of bitter division. On its eve, the Levellers issued a pamphlet, *A Call to All the Soldiers of the Army by the Free People of England*, which vigorously attacked Cromwell and Ireton for their 'hypocrisy' and 'deceit'. Of Cromwell they wrote that he was once loved as 'just, honest, sincere and valiant', placing 'the country and the liberties of the people above his life', hating the King 'as a man of blood'; but now, if he did not instantly repent, he should 'cease to be the object of your love'. They said that Ireton by his imperious carriage had made the Army Council 'like unto Star Chambers'. 'None but flatterers, tale-bearers and turncoats are countenanced by him.'

For fourteen days the parliament of the army argued, at first in hot temper leading to a morning of prayer to subdue the temperature, afterwards engaged in a fundamental conflict of principles. The Agitators brought with them two civilian Levellers, one of whom, John Wildman, was destined through fifty years and five reigns to assist the Republican cause – 'the soul of English politics', Disraeli called him. The chief protagonists were Ireton on the conservative side, clear-cut, logical, superior; Rainsborough, forthright, moving, with the common touch, on the radical side. For the Agitators, Private Sexby was blunt and belligerent, often unanswerable. Cromwell characteristically sought to explain and excuse, but left the main debating to Ireton.

The social difference between generals and men was revealed in a long debate on the basis of citizenship. The ranks and indeed many officers argued for manhood suffrage, the generals for a suffrage representing property. Rainsborough put the case for human equality:

The poorest he that is in England hath a life to live, as the greatest he; and therefore, truly, Sir, I think it's clear that every man that is to live under a government ought first by his own consent to put himself under that government; and I do think that the poorest man in England is not at all bound in a strict sense to that government that he hath not had a voice to put himself under.

Arguing for a property qualification, Ireton replied:

No person hath a right to an interest or share in the disposing of the affairs of the kingdom, and in determining or choosing those that shall determine what laws we shall be ruled by here – no person hath a right to this that hath not a permanent fixed interest in this kingdom.

As the debate went on, it became clear that the spokesmen for property feared that the enfranchisement of the property-less would lead to confiscation. Said Ireton:

If you admit any man that hath a breath and being...this will destroy property...Why may not these men vote against all property?

The radicals began to suggest that property was theft and the instrument of privilege and power. Said Rainsborough:

I am a poor man therefore I must be pressed [conscripted by gangs]; if I have no interest in the kingdom, I must suffer by all their laws...Gentlemen with three or four lordships (God knows how they got them) can always get into Parliament and evict the poor from their homes. I would fane know whether the potency of rich men do not this, and so keep them [the poor] under the greatest tyranny that was ever thought of in the world.

Although the debate had so largely gone against the generals, the committee entrusted to draft conclusions, while representative in its composition, produced proposals weighted heavily on the conservative side. (How this happened is not known. Did the Agitators fail to attend, or was this an example of the power of the machine?) The traditional franchise was to remain, though in addition votes would be given to all who had fought for the Parliament or had helped its cause in the Civil War. The demand for religious toleration was watered down so that while a magistrate could no longer force a dissenter to attend a Presbyterian Church, he could still prevent any body of believers of whom the government disapproved – Episcopalian, Catholic, Jew, Baptist, Congregationalist – from meeting to worship in their own fashions. Pressganging to conscript men for the forces was forbidden for overseas service, but was specifically sanctioned for the defence of England, or 'keeping the peace within it'. Moreover, the basic idea of the *Agreement*, that its authority should arise from the people and should override the powers of Parliament, was dismissed. Instead, the document was to be forwarded to Parliament as suggestions, although it was laid down that several of the clauses should be unalterable and not subject to abrogation by the Commons. What happened in detail when these recommendations came before the full council we do not know – the reports are incomplete – but it is recorded that suffrage for all adults, 'if they be not servants or beggars' (Lilburne's formula), was carried against Cromwell and Ireton with only three dissentients, and the fact that the Agitators voted for the final *Agreement* to be submitted to a recalled rendezvous of the whole army suggests that it was not in principle unacceptable to them.

The generals outwitted the Agitators. Instead of calling one national rendezvous, which would have given the troops a sense of united solidarity influenced by leaders like Rainsborough, they summoned three regional rendezvous. Conflict arose before they met. A council meeting from which Cromwell was absent decided to send a letter to the Speaker of the Commons making clear that the army did not agree with Ireton when he had opposed a motion that no further addresses be made to the King. The letter made no mention of Ireton, but he took mortal offence, saying he would withdraw from the council until it was repudiated. At the next meeting Cromwell from the chair made a forthright attack on the Agitators, complaining of the communication to the Speaker. A resolution which he proposed was carried that the officers and the Agitators should immediately return to their regiments to quieten the distemper among the men.

The next day in the council, with Fairfax, usually impartial, presiding, a resolution to satisfy Ireton was adopted. This stated that the army was not against further approaches to the King, and the Speaker was so informed. The generals were steadily outmanoeuvring the Agitators. To lessen the frustration among all ranks, they begged Parliament in an urgent prayer for six (or at least four) weeks' pay to soften the injustice of arrears still unpaid. They then thought of the idea of preparing a manifesto for submission to the regional rendezvous, pledging loyalty and discipline by the troops. How could soldiers under an oath reject that? More intimidatingly, they began the manifesto by announcing that General Fairfax, generally revered for his fairness, would resign his Command if the manifesto were not accepted.

An event now occurred which brought unity behind the generals. The King escaped to the Isle of Wight from Hampton Court, where he had been transferred after the army entered London. There was little doubt that his motive was to gain freedom to plan cooperation with the Scots in a renewed war for his restoration to the throne. The effect was to close ranks within the army, and to rally the men behind their military leaders. The payment of their arrears was important, manhood suffrage and religious toleration were important, but these must wait until the threat from the 'man of blood' was removed. In fact, Parliament went some way to reduce resentment among the men. A promise was made to raise £20,000 towards meeting arrears, and John Lilburne was given permission to leave his prison by day without a 'keeper' so that he should be free to prepare his defence.

John used his liberty to ride to Ware, where, in the inn, he waited for news from neighbouring Corkbush Field, the meeting place of the most important regional rendezvous. The news when it came was disastrous. There was at the outset some affray between Rainsborough and Fairfax, apparently not serious, when the Leveller presented the commander with a petition in favour of the original *Agreement* and the commander brushed it aside. Soon a graver conflict arose. A rebellious officer, Colonel Eyres, and a dissenting M.P., Major Scott, distributed copies of *The Agreement* among the soldiers and were arrested for insinuating 'seditious privileges into the soldiers, incensing them against the General and the general officers'. Meanwhile two regiments, one led by John Lilburne's brother, Robert, insisted on attending the Ware rendezvous although allocated to another. They wore in their hats copies of *The Agreement* bearing the slogan 'England's Freedom, Soldiers' Rights'. Fairfax thereupon addressed a severe reproof to the regiments, one of which agreed to obey his commands to retire. Lilburne's refused. They drew up, 'as if they had been going to engage with an enemy,' and declined to remove the white papers in their hats when commanded. 'Whereupon some officers rode in among them and plucked out the papers of some of them that were most insolent and then the rest began to submit.' The 'most insolent', however, continued to resist and swords were drawn; this was mutiny, and it was severely repressed. Three men were tried on the spot by court martial and sentenced to death. They were allowed to throw dice for their lives. The man who lost, Private Richard Arnold, was shot at the head of the regiment. 'So ended the mutiny at Ware,' comments Brailsford.

The rendezvous continued its proceedings, adopting a *Remonstrance* denouncing attacks on the generals and declaring that if they were not stopped General Fairfax would resign. If, however, discipline were restored, he would do his utmost to get Parliament to meet the soldiers' grievances on pay and to provide for the disabled, widows and orphans. A list of proposals followed for the reform of Parliament, although no mention was made of the veto of the King and the Lords. Religious toleration was forgotten. The *Remonstrance* was a defeat for the Agitators and Levellers. Further courts martial were held to try the mutineers. Six of Robert Lilburne's regiment suffered the brutal punishment of running the gauntlet, beaten, bare-backed, as they ran between two ranks of soldiers, Robert was not himself arrested, and courageously denounced the treatment of his fellows, asserting that the taking of life by martial law in time of peace amounted to murder.

Then came an event perhaps even more decisive than the King's escape in overcoming disunity in the army. There were the beginnings of a definite shift in Cromwell's attitude to the King when, at a meeting of the army's General Council at

Windsor Castle on 4 December 1647, he expressed regret for persevering too long in negotiating with the monarch, saying that 'the glories of the world had so dazzled his eyes, that . . . he was now resolved to humble himself', and that he desired 'the prayers of the Saints that God would be pleased to forgive him his self-seeking'. Cromwell's decisive abandonment of all attempts to negotiate with Charles I came with the vehement speech he made in the Commons on 3 January 1648, supporting a successful motion that no addresses should be made to the King. In this he described Charles I as 'a dissembler and so false a man that he was not to be trusted'.

Meanwhile his revision of attitude had been accompanied by reconciliation within the army. There was on 21 December 1647 the customary day of prayer and fasting which brought 'sweet harmony', Cromwell, Ireton and other officers praying 'very fervently and pathetically from nine in the morning to seven at night'. All the sentences on the mutineers were quashed, and they were restored to their posts on undertaking to observe discipline; the Levellers expressed regret for their indiscretions at Ware. At the conclusion of the meeting, General Fairfax invited all the members to dine with him in the castle, where they congratulated each other on the unity achieved.

The Agitators won the council over to accepting many of their demands. At the Windsor meeting it was agreed to send to the Commons an impressive deputation of seven colonels, 'with other officers of rank and quality', to assure Parliament that it would support action to settle 'the Kingdom without the King and against him', a view which the Agitators, defying the wishes of Cromwell and Ireton, had expressed to the Speaker two months before. They had won their main demand, but they were soon to lose their power. Having regained the confidence of the ranks, the generals reasserted their authority. Fairfax refrained from summoning the Agitators to the next meeting of the council and it became clear that he had no intention of doing so in future. When one regiment protested, the Levellers revived the call for representation, but the generals reacted strongly. They arrested and imprisoned the two privates who conveyed the petition from the regiment and threatened them with death. The men were released, but the participation of the Agitators in decision-making was over. Why? On May Day 1648 the Second Civil War began. Democracy in the army was ended.

Part Two:
The Rise and Fall of the Levellers, 1649–57

The Levellers were of historic importance not only for their democratic demands; they were the first political group of which we have knowledge to be organized on a democratic basis. From John Lilburne we learn its pattern. Each member paid a subscription according to income, varying from twopence to half a crown a week, which only the better-off tradesmen could afford. The local units were attached to a neighbourly tavern, each electing representatives to district committees, which in turn elected twelve commissioners who decided the tactics of the party and two treasurers who kept its war chest. At first this organization was confined to the City and to London suburbs. Activities when the party spread in the country are indicated in a letter Lilburne addressed to sympathizers in Kent, asking them to attend a meeting at Dartford to be followed by a demonstration at the House of Commons which adherents from all the Home Counties would swell.

The executive committee met in the evening, according to Lilburne, as often as three times a week at the Whalebone Tavern in the City, and on one evening a week at other

Leveller taverns in Southwark, Wapping and Shoreditch. The Whalebone was the party headquarters, and the host, we are told, would always receive signatures to the petitions. Petitions, often containing 30,000 signatures, and pamphlets were the principal methods of propaganda. Funds were mainly devoted to meeting the heavy cost of paper. The printing was done clandestinely at the presses of members until the party had its own press at Oxford. The pamphlets were illegal, the Stationers' Company having monopoly rights of publication, but bands of voluntary distributors secured wide circulation. It was probably the King who gave the Levellers their name, 'a most apt title' remarked his chronicler, Marchemont Nedham, 'for such a despicable and desperate knot to be known by, that endeavour to cast down and level the enclosures of nobility, gentry and propriety, to make us all even, so that every Jack shall vie with a gentleman and every gentleman be made a Jack'. The Levellers appeared to be less puritanical and self-righteous than many of the sects with whom they cooperated in opposition to the Presbyterians. It was their custom when the men in the army suffered physical punishment to take them in a coach for a feast at the Whalebone. The stricter Baptists made a practice of concluding their petitions to Parliament by calling for the severe punishment of swearing, drunkenness and wenching. In no Leveller petitions do we find this moral superiority condemning the sins of the unrighteous. They were not profligate, but were content to be positive in their manner of life rather than censorious of others.

The Levellers not only inspired many of the Agitators' army demands, they served as the propagandists for them among the civilian population. Often this was risky. When a decision was taken at the Whalebone Tavern to send a deputation to Parliament to urge an inquiry into the circumstances of the death of Private Arnold at Ware, five of the London leaders were imprisoned 'during the pleasure of this House'. Before the end of 1646, Parliament – bracketing the party with Royalists who had invaded the House in July – set out to deprive known Levellers of the right to vote for the London Common Council or the right to be elected to it – an indication of the fear in which their growing strength was held. This fear was also shown in concessions made. There was strong resentment among the tradesmen of London, whom the Levellers largely represented, of the immunities which members of both Houses of Parliament enjoyed (even having the right to extend them to their dependants and servants) when claims were made against them of failure to meet financial obligations. Parliament agreed to abolish these privileges, though it still protected members from imprisonment for debt. A second attempt to meet Leveller-aroused opinion was the appointment of a commission to review all undertakings related to 'the people's burdens, freedoms and liberties', including measures for the reform of the courts and legal procedure, and – could terms of reference be much broader? – to 'all other things of public concernment which they should hold fit and reasonable for the good and weal of the people'. Nothing came from the commission. It was only a gesture to quieten the popularity of the Levellers' campaign on legal and social wrongs.

The year 1647 was one of economic distress. There was a bad harvest and production slowed down because of the fear of the renewal of civil war. In London there was much hardship. Parliament at last set up a 'Corporation of the Poor' under the chairmanship of the Lord Mayor, composed of fifty-eight top officials, with the aim of initiating a housing programme 'to set the poor to work', but the plan failed. The Poor Law ceased to operate and starvation spread over the country. In Wiltshire, unemployed weavers seized corn on the way to market and divided it among themselves. The general mood elsewhere, however, was one of despair rather than revolution.

The Levellers were deeply moved by the misery they saw around them. Their petition to Parliament for the first time included an economic programme. Brailsford judged that John Lilburne was the author. Who else would have said that the suffering of the people was due to 'the devouring fire of the Lord's wrath'? But the contents of the petition suggest that Overton collaborated. There was the usual political introduction, which embraced some interesting new proposals. Lilburne had evidently got the Levellers' executive to accept manhood suffrage since it appears (with his limitations), but most noteworthy is the emphasis on decentralization and participation. Not only was Overton's idea that magistrates should be elected annually in each parish adopted, but this principle was extended to juries and even to the 'committee men' responsible for local administration. Later the Levellers added the church minister and regimental militia officers to those subject to election. In a sentence, the Levellers' proposals would have destroyed the domination of the landowners as the ruling class in the countryside, so promoting a rural revolution. The petition also broke new ground in advocating for the first time on record the separation of the judiciary from government.

But it was the economic programme, Overton's speciality, which was most relevant to the situation in town and country. It was prefaced by the broad requirement that 'the too long continued shame of this nation, namely permission of any to suffer such poverty as to beg their bread, be effectively ended'. The actual proposals were a little vague (like modern exhortations to greater effort), but their implications in participation were drastic. The demand was made that the poor be given the right to choose representatives to control 'stocks, houses, land, etc., which of right belong to them and their use'. The word 'stocks' here refers to money and materials which were provided in a parish for the employment or relief of the poor, so the apparently wide scope for democratic control which a modern eye might read into the passage is not in fact relevant.

The second item in the programme is, on a broader basis, 'forthwith to advance the native commodities of this nation', the products of the field, which the greater part of the population was cultivating. There was no suggestion of how this should be done, but it was a priority for recovery. Thirdly,

John Lilburne on the pillory after his trial at the Star Chamber in 1638

A contemporary engraving, by Wenceslaus Hollar, of the Tower of London, scene of Lilburne's imprisonment on several occasions

Coll. John Lilborne.

Nil Admirari

MAJOR IOHN WILDMAN.

THREE LEADING LEVELLERS:

John Lilburne

John Wildman

Thomas Rainsborough

COL. RAINSBOROUGH

THREE LEADING PARLIAMENTARIANS:

Oliver Cromwell

Henry Ireton

Thomas Lord Fairfax

THOMAS LORD FAIRFAX

Putney Parish Church, scene of the Putney Debates in 1647

A contemporary impression of this historic meeting
in Putney of General Fairfax and the Military Council

Another Leveller leader, Richard Overton, was incarcerated in Newgate (*above*) 'among stink and vermin', while his wife was held in Bridewell (*below*), 'amongst bawds and strumpets'

The trial of Charles I in 1649

The Death Warrant of Charles I, from an engraving

Burford Church: Interior (*above*) – the Leveller inspired mutiny in the army in 1649 led to the arrest of 340 Levellers within the Church. The font (*below*) – an inscription by one of these prisoners

A nineteenth-century impression of Cromwell dissolving the
Long Parliament in 1653, by Benjamin West (1738-1820)

manufactures should be improved 'for the advantage of our own mariners and the whole nation'. Again there was no indication of the means to achieve this, but it is interesting that there should have been such a reference to trade abroad as well as home production. Finally came the very relevant demand that the poor should have 'better wages for their labour'.

In more vigorous language but less constructively, the Levellers then addressed the army. They entitled their letter *The Mournful Cries of Many Thousand Poor Tradesmen, who are ready to Famish through Decay of Trade, or the Warning Tears of the Oppressed*. To the Commons and the City they said, 'O you Members of Parliament and rich men in the City, that are at ease and drink wine in bowls and stretch yourselves upon beds of down, you that grind our faces and flay off our skins, will no man amongst you regard, will no man behold our faces black with sorrow and famine?' A passionate appeal is made for peace as necessary to remedy distress (the Second Civil War had not yet begun) and the troops are implored to join 'the perishing people' in telling Commoners and Lords that 'the tears of the oppressed will wash away the foundations of their houses'.

In January 1648, Lilburne was again arrested. The minister of the Presbyterian church at Shoreditch attended a meeting which he and Wildman addressed at Wapping, and he was so shocked by Leveller teaching that he reported to Parliament what he heard. Without waiting for a warrant, Lilburne and Wildman presented themselves at the House of Commons to reply to the parson's charges. The debate which followed went on until candles were brought in, ending with the verdict that the two Levellers had been guilty of 'treasonable and seditious practices against the state'. Orders were given that Lilburne should again be confined in the Tower and Wildman in the Fleet prison. The intrepid Lilburne immediately challenged the orders. Waiting in the lobby with a hundred followers, he convinced the Serjeant-at-Arms that the Speaker's warrant was wrongly drafted and he was allowed to go free on giving his parole. Next morning, although the warrant had been amended, Lilburne still insisted that it was out of order because it did not mention any particular act of treason, and he browbeat the guard, officers and men so successfully that they declined to lay hands on him. Not so a colonel who then arrived. He ordered the soldiers to draw their swords and to attack the resisting Lilburne – once more it was his wife Elizabeth who saved his life by flinging herself between his body and the raised weapons. Lilburne was carried to the Tower.

Parliament decided to crush the Levellers. In the City and Tower Hamlets the militia was ordered to break up all their meetings, and similiar instructions were sent to the county committees of Kent. There is some evidence that the Levellers then began to think of armed defence. In a pamphlet, *A New Engagement*, they write of the necessity to 'put themselves into a posture of defending their own and the country's liberties' and appeal to serving soldiers and ex-soldiers for support. That they foresaw armed conflict is indicated in the promise that they would 'gladly and cheerfully return to our private habitations and callings' when demands were met. The confrontation did not arise. The Second Civil War broke and brought a severer conflict with new allies.

The war characteristically took a religious form. Only by the spilling of blood, it was urged, could the earth be cleansed from the stain of blood. Yet it was fought with a brutality and tyranny to which the Parliament's armies in the First Civil War rarely descended. Now, when Royalist commanders surrendered, they were shot. More shocking, because it was done in cold blood, prisoners were sold as slaves to cotton masters in America and the Caribbean islands. Brailsford tells that one 'lot' of Scots was offered to the Most Catholic King of Spain and the Most Christian King of France, but the cash required was not forthcoming. Evidence indicates that the majority of the English people favoured the King, but Cromwell's skill as a general and his ruthlessness won him battle after battle.

When the first enthusiasm of the war passed, the ranks in the forces, although they had been deprived of their representatives on the Army Council, began boldly to express their grievances again. They did so in language reminiscent of the dismissed Agitators. Two regiments of horse troops, for example, hotly protested against their treatment. They recollected how, at the beginning of the war, they were regarded as the saviours of the nation. Their chaplains told them 'that if a man died in this service his soul was in heaven before his blood was cold in his body'. But now 'all that Parliament does for us is to set the churchwardens of the parishes in London to beg for us at the church doors'. They didn't hesitate to voice the contrast: 'But if any Member of Parliament suffers loss the House at once votes him thousands of pounds for his loss of hundreds.' They went on to call for the re-establishment of an Army Council, composed of two representatives from each county and two from each regiment. Here was evidence that the influence of the Agitators and the Levellers was still very much alive in the army.

Although Parliament had declared war on the King, it became, like the City, increasingly Royalist-minded. By 165 votes to 99, it decided that government should continue to be 'by King, Lords and Commons'. It withdrew the earlier decision to exclude Holles and his Royalist colleagues, and the Lords twice rejected a resolution that persons who adhered to the Scottish invaders should be proceeded against as rebels and traitors. Worse was to follow. An Ordinance was passed establishing the Presbyterian system of church government throughout England without tolerance towards other denominations; the earlier decision that no further addresses should be made to the King was repealed; and, after much pressure from the City, whose Common Council declared for peace at any price, negotiations with the King were authorized and begun at Newport.

The call of the City for peace was not entirely the result of Royalist pressure. It reflected the fact that the metropolis was under seige through the blocking of all trade up the Thames by a naval force commanded by the King's son, later to be Charles II. The earlier distress was aggravated. The London

Levellers reacted with a pamphlet published under the long but explicit title, *England's Troublers Troubled, on the Just Resolutions of the Plain Men of England against the Rich and Mighty, by whose Pride, Treachery and Wilfulness they are brought into Extreme Necessity and Misery*. The author may have been Henry Marten, the Republican M.P. Marten, while not himself a Leveller, was, of course, against the King – indeed, he raised a regiment of horse in his constituency – but he was also against those, other than the military commanders, who were supposed to be conducting the war. He wrote that the men of property were responsible for everything that had gone wrong.

'Ye have [he declared], by corruption in government, by unjust and unequal laws, by fraud, cosenage, tyranny and oppression, gotten most of the land of this distressed and enslaved nation into your ravenous claws. Ye have by monopolies, usurers and combinations engrossed all the wealth, monies and houses into your possessions; yea and enclosed our commons in most counties.'

Rarely has exploitation been more strongly denounced.

The decisions of Parliament listed above caused confusion about the purpose of the war. 'What are we fighting for?' men began to ask. William Walwyn wrote a pamphlet, *The Bloody Project*, which expressed these doubts. Neither the King nor Parliament had made clear the terms for which they professed to be fighting. 'To be short, all the quarrel we have at this day in the kingdom,' he wrote, 'is no other than a quarrel of interests and parties, a pulling down of one tyrant to set up another, and instead of liberty, heaping upon ourselves a greater slavery than that we fought against.' This distrust, equally of the establishment and of the King, led him almost to the pacifist position. 'You must note that you are a free people, and are not to be pressed to serve in wars like horses and brute beasts. . .,' he insisted. 'It is not sufficient to fight by lawful authority, but you must be sure to fight for what is just.' He concluded:

All you soldiers and people that have your consciences alive
about you [should seek] to prevent a further effusion of
blood.... The King, Parliament, great men in the City and
the Army have made you but the stairs by which they have
mounted to honour, wealth and power. The only quarrel
that hath been and at present is but this, namely whose
slaves the people shall be.

The Levellers were moving towards an attitude, even in a war
ostensibly against the monarchy, of a 'plague on both your
houses'.

Something unexpected happened. When, three months
after the outbreak of the war, the Levellers presented to
Parliament a petition signed by over 10,000 for the release of
John Lilburne from the Tower, one of Denzil Holles's group,
Sir John Maynard, after paying an astonishingly warm eulogy
to 'this brave invincible spirit', moved that the sentence be
cancelled. More astonishingly, Parliament consented. The
next day Lilburne was freed. This was not as irrational as it
seemed. The Presbyterians and Royalists in Parliament
wished to encourage the neutralist tendency among the Levellers, holding that it would weaken support for the war against
the King; and they hoped that Lilburne, because of past
suffering at his hands, would join their attack on Cromwell
whom they proposed to impeach for treason. The Leveller
leader disappointed them. He would have nothing to do with
the impeachment of a general whose army was all that stood
between not only the restoration of an unrestricted Charles
but the episcopal intolerance of the Presbyterian Church.
Lilburne sent by forced marches a self-confident but generous
message to Cromwell, who was campaigning in the North.

If [he wrote] I...desired revenge for an hard and almost
starving imprisonment, I could have had of late the choice
of twenty opportunities to have paid you to the purpose;
but I scorn it, especially when you are low...If ever my
hand be upon you, it shall be when you are in your full

glory, if then you shall decline from the righteous ways of truth and justice – which if you will fixedly and impartially prosecute, I am yours to the last drop of my heart blood (for all your late severe hand towards me).

Cromwell, despite the opposition in Parliament and the City, was soon to prove that he was not 'low'. He overwhelmed the Royalist forces at Preston, and with the army at his command became the power in the land. Hastily Parliament backed down from its motion of impeachment. How opportunist it was! There now arose an alliance between the Levellers and the Cromwellian Puritans. Sexby carried on his role of go-between by taking Lilburne's message to Cromwell and returned with the commander's welcoming reply – unfortunately verbal, so we know only its spirit. Encouraged, the Levellers drew up a comprehensive programme, *The Large Petition of 11 September*, which they hoped Cromwell would endorse. It was a compromise document, omitting extreme demands such as manhood suffrage, repeating the known political aims, emphasizing religious tolerance, requiring one law for high and low, rejecting conscription, abolishing the monopolist companies, throwing open the 'recent enclosures' of fens and commons. To the disappointment of the left among the Levellers the programme proceeded to insist that Parliament 'and all future Parliaments' were bound to refrain 'from abolishing property, levelling man's estates, and making all things common' – thus ending the tendency in the Levellers to become prototypes for egalitarian socialists. *The Large Petition* was enthusiastically welcomed by the army. Without waiting for the approval of the generals, a crowd of junior officers invaded the House of Commons and called for a reply.

Parliament recognized the status which the Levellers had gained by publishing what we should term a Green Paper rejecting its principles. This document was important in its revelation of the divorce between Cromwell and the Presbyterians. For one thing, it openly avowed the divine right of

Kings. 'We are called by the King's writ,' they wrote, 'not to redress grievances but to present them.' While it was admitted that Parliament's consent was necessary to what 'The King shall please to enact', the sovereignty of the people was rejected. The King was accountable to none but God only. 'You are exceedingly deceived in that you say that all authority is derived from the people, for God gives the King his authority...To deny the negative of the King and Lords were robbery...rebellion and disobedience.' Parliament had only the power to consent to things ordained by common council, 'that is by the King with the advice of the Lords'. The Green Paper concluded by insisting that, 'There must be an end of war and God's and the King's mercy implored.' The battle was joined between autocracy and democracy.

The Levellers' *Large Petition* received massive backing in the country. Encouraged by a nationwide sale of *The Moderate*, the party's paper, towns poured supporting petitions on Parliament. At Newcastle-upon-Tyne, eighty-four leading citizens signed, including the mayor, aldermen, sherriffs, and members of the Common Council. The queue of petitioners included Bristol, Hull, York, and the counties of Cornwall, Somerset, Oxford, Leicester, Berkshire and Wiltshire. There was even greater support from the army, regiments dispatching petitions in rapid succession, the more remarkable because they were signed, as was the rule after the dispersal of the Agitators, by the officers on behalf of all ranks.

The official attitude of the army was decided at a council held in the choir of the Abbey of St Albans in November. Attendance was limited to officers, the practice since the suppression of regimental representation. Ireton came out in favour of the King's execution. Fairfax, on the other hand, was strongly in favour of the existing kingdom, and said that if the negotiations at Newport led to a treaty, he would defend Parliament and King. His view was decisive, and Ireton was left almost alone. Cromwell was, at the time, leading his troops from Preston to Durham, and there is no record of his presence, but he was probably wavering. There is no doubt, however, that opinion in the ranks was radical.

It is time to mention something about the negotiations at Newport between Parliament and King, but the truth is that there is little to say. They dragged on, the King devious, never trustworthy in any concessions because he held that, restored to God's authority as monarch, he could disavow promises made under duress. He seemed most concerned to make peace in England in order to press another war, the crushing of resistance to Westminster's rule in Ireland.

An incident occurred this autumn which meant a great personal loss to the Levellers, but which led to an extraordinary proof of their strength in popular opinion. After the spectacular capture of Colchester by Rainsborough, he was transferred north to reduce the nearly impregnable fortress of Pontefract. Early one Sunday morning he received in his quarters at Doncaster two visitors who claimed that they brought a message from Cromwell. They were disguised Royalists and, finding the general unarmed, compelled him to go with them. In the street Rainsborough attacked his captors with his naked hands and fought until he had been run through several times. The Levellers were shattered by the loss of their brave voice within the army, yet were inspired by the demonstration of devotion which it evoked. The funeral bier from Tottenham High Cross to the chapel at Wapping was followed by the most impressive procession London had seen. First came women in fifty coaches, then troopers on horseback, estimated between 1,500 and 3,000, and finally greater masses of mourners, described by the Royalist *Mercuries* as 'Will the weaver, Tom the tapster, Kit the cobbler, Dick the door-sweeper, and many more eminent apron-youths of the City.' Everyone wore ribbons of sea-green, Rainsborough's colours, which from this day became the Levellers' badge. The immense popular influence of the Levellers now became clear even to Parliament and the City as well as to the commanding officers in the army.

From this moment negotiations began for an alliance between Cromwell and his associates and the Levellers. On the suggestion of Cromwell, influential supporters among Baptists and Congregationalists as well as senior officers met Lilburne and his close comrades at the Nag's Head, Holloway. On the morrow, Ireton, appreciating that he must recruit allies, met the Levellers at Windsor. Sexby, in his customary role, went to see Cromwell at Pontefract, where he had taken over the siege duties of Rainsborough. Cromwell agreed to meet Henry Marten, the republican M.P., and sent separately for Lilburne. This time the Levellers' leader and Cromwell did not get on well. The negotiations between them broke down. 'Things about him. . .savoured more of intended self-exalting than. . .the advancement of the. . .liberties and freedoms of the nation,' remarked the Leveller of the general. Cromwell, distant from London, was not convinced that the Levellers were strong enough to exert any considerable influence. He referred to their extreme demands and dismissed them with the remark 'of whom there is no fear'.

Then followed an event which appears to have converted Cromwell to the need to purge Parliament of its Royalist sympathizers, a step which Ireton had for some time urged. In Scotland, the Committee of Estates, virtually a national parliament, within which there was a majority of supporters of the King, was dissolved by the troops of the Duke of Argyll who had deserted Charles's ranks. Cromwell fastened on this as a precedent. 'A lesser party of Parliament hath made it lawful to declare the greater part a faction,' he commented, and added significantly, 'Think of the example. . .and let others think of it, too.' The Levellers, however, opposed a restriction of Parliament to 'the Saints'. At the meeting with the divines at the Stag's Head, Lilburne argued that they would be at the mercy of the army, which would be cozened by the generals as it had been before. He urged the acceptance of *The Agreement of the People* to secure a democratic Parliament. The representatives of the dissident churches and the senior officers at first favoured the purge, but Lilburne's vigour and magnetic personality actually won their consent for *The Agreement*.

At a second meeting, attended by four delegates from each side, Lilburne's proposals carried. There was deadlock at the beginning, a certain Rev. John Price declining to participate with William Walwyn, perhaps because he was too pacifist. The difficulty was resolved by both retiring. It was agreed unanimously that a convention should be called of all concerned, including the army, to prepare a contract 'above the law' which should lay down the 'limits and extent' of the powers of Parliament, the revolutionary constitutional idea which the Levellers had earlier put forward.

There were still some differences between the Levellers and the élite Army Council. To resolve these, a third meeting was held at the Garton Inn, Windsor, to seek accord with Ireton, who had formulated the council's view in a detailed petition, *The Remonstrance*. At first discussion failed, Ireton rejecting the Levellers' view of religious liberty. While prepared to deny any coercive powers to the state, he would retain its restrictive powers, not tolerating Episcopalians, Catholics, Unitarians and Jews. A difference also emerged regarding the judicial powers of Parliament. Because Charles could not be charged under any existing law, Ireton proposed that Parliament should be given the right to penalize 'according to their own judgement'. This outraged Lilburne's principles, a perilous precedent. He prepared to quit, but was persuaded to attend a second discussion. At this Lilburne gave way on the Leveller proposal for a convention to prepare *The Agreement of the People*. Instead he agreed to a representative committee, with four members each from the army, the dissident churches, the dependable M.P.s and the Levellers.

Meanwhile, however, Fairfax and his Army Council of officers offered to the King his restoration on an assurance that there should be the dissolution of the Long Parliament, a regular succession of Parliaments, a redistribution of seats, state control of the militia, and the surrender of the right of the Monarch to appoint the officers of the Crown. No mention was made of the King's veto of legislation or religious toleration. The terms were unexpectedly conciliatory, but

Charles rejected them. Fairfax and his council thereupon endorsed Ireton's *Remonstrance*, which doomed the King to be put on trial, and when Parliament postponed a decision indefinitely, Fairfax issued an ultimation that it would be purged. He invited those Members of Parliament 'as God kept upright' to separate themselves from those who had betrayed their trust. They were promised that the army would 'own them, adhere to them, and be guided by them in their faithful prosecution of that trust'.

Parliament damned itself. Acting on its own standard of political morality, it tried to buy off the army by instructing the Lord Mayor to fund £40,000 due from the City towards arrears of pay. Fairfax showed his contempt by ordering the troops to march on London, and on 5 December 1648 troops under Colonel Pride excluded from the Commons some ninety Members belonging to the Presbyterian majority. The forty-five who resisted were arrested, most released after three days, though three leading recalcitrants were kept in the Tower untried for some years. Holles escaped to the Continent. Pride carried out his purge without the explicit authority of Fairfax or Cromwell, but there is no doubt that he had the backing of the whole army. The Levellers opposed the continuation of the Parliament under the rule of the 'Saints'. It had been there for eight years without any submissions to the people and should be dissolved. But the truth was probably that, if Parliament had been dissolved, a majority of the electors would have voted for Charles.

The alliance between the Levellers and the army was wrecked over the issue of religious toleration. A meeting of the Army Council was held to which representatives of the dissident churches and of the Levellers were invited, though no Agitators were present to speak for the ranks. Ireton (and he expressed the view of Cromwell) accepted the view that the state should not impose religious beliefs, but he insisted that Parliament and the magistrates should have the right to restrict the public profession of belief and the practice of worship. The Levellers refused to accept this denial of conscience. As Liberals, they passionately opposed the tyranny of the Presbyterians who had imposed heavy fines if dissidents failed to attend the established churches, and who even seized the children of Catholics in order that they should be brought up as Protestants. The celebration of the Mass was a criminal offence for which a priest might be hanged and his flock imprisoned. Courageously the Levellers stood firmly for the liberty of Catholics, Jews, Unitarians and atheists as well as of Baptists and Congregationalists. Tribute for this should be paid to them. They were the first party anywhere in the world outside the Netherlands who declared for toleration without qualification. At this meeting of the Army Council they were outvoted. The revised *Agreement of the People*, which the army adopted, inserted Ireton's view. The Levellers published their own version – and withdrew.

The Rump Parliament of the 'Saints' put Charles on trial and executed him. Lilburne rejected an invitation to sit as one of the judges of the High Court which condemned the King to death. He had been the first in January 1647 in his pamphlet *Regal Tyranny Discovered* to call for the trial and execution of Charles, but, liberal always, he took the view that the 'mock Parliament', the Rump, was not entitled to try the monarch. He wished action to be postponed until *The Agreement of the People* had been adopted and a new Parliament had been democratically elected. The King, Lilburne urged, was entitled like every other citizen to be tried in one of the accepted courts before twelve jurymen. His outraged sense of justice was so great that he offered help to three Royalists in their defence. He had no sympathy with what they had done, but held that they were entitled to trial before a regular court.

There were divided opinions among the Leveller leaders. Overton unreservedly approved the execution of Charles as 'the supremest piece of justice that ever was in England'. Walwyn regretted the killing since the King was a 'hereditary' tyrant, having learned his doctrine of God-given power from his father; it was therefore an injustice 'to take away his life for his parents' sin'. Nevertheless, he believed the 'tyrant's end' would prove historically valuable as a warning to later monarchs. Henry Marten, Sexby and Wildman deserted the party, the first to become one of the leaders of the Rump, the second to become one of Cromwell's favourites in his army, the third in pursuit of his career independently. The truth is that the Levellers went into temporary vacation. Lilburne retreated to Durham, seeking to collect from the estates of delinquents the compensation which Parliament had voted for his sufferings under the Star Chamber. Of the £3,000 due, he gathered £600.

The retirement of the Levellers was short. The Rump Parliament soon became tyrannical. It faced appalling economic depression with four times as many persons as usual in need of relief. Unemployment spread in both the countryside and in the towns. The Levellers' paper, *The Moderate*, printed reports from many districts. 'We have not bread to put in our mouths . . . The poor are almost famished,' was recorded from Lancaster. Lilburne asked to address the government from the bar. Thinking of the impoverished peasantry, he made a strong plea for the abolition of tithes forthwith. Such a gesture, he urged, would demonstrate the new attitude of the rulers and 'so fasten you in the affections of the people and of the honest officers and soldiers, as that you should not need to fear any opposite power whatsoever'. The Rump did not respond. Henry Marten did introduce a Bill to end imprisonment for debt, but it was made inoperative by lawyers' obstruction. Anger spread in the forces when Parliament set the pressgang in motion to conscript men for the navy. In the words of the Levellers as summarized by Brailsford, '"the plain man" was soon murmuring that though the King was beheaded, nothing in his own daily round was changed'.

The Levellers were particularly outraged when Parliament reintroduced the censorship of publications in a severer form than the Presbyterians had practised. The object was to suppress unlicensed pamphlets. Fines or imprisonment were imposed on author, printer and bookseller, the offending press was to be seized and dismantled, and any pedlar who sold the pamphlets was to be whipped as a common rogue. Moreover, Fairfax was instructed to make full use of his military police to enforce the ordinance. The Levellers protested in a well-written petition which boldly vindicated the freedom of the press. It reminded the Commons that they would never have dared to proclaim the sovereignty of the people (which they had just ironically done) had not the Levellers prepared the way by their unlicensed pamphlets. It denounced the punishment of whipping, 'fit only for slaves or bondmen', and with emphasis protested against the setting up of 'a military jurisdiction' which they desired to avoid for ever and above everything in the world. This was the first blow in a campaign against military dictatorship which, from this point, became the major theme of the Levellers.

The next step was audacious. The Levellers initiated a petition within the army calling for less severe discipline, the reduction of martial law and the abolition of controls over civilian life (exemplified by enforcing pamphlet censorship). The High Command were indignant that civilians should meddle with discipline in the army, and Fairfax prohibited any petitions without his own final permission. Cromwell and Ireton as Members of Parliament were asked by their fellow generals to promote legislation to inflict upon civilians who 'breed division in the army' the same punishment which they would suffer if in the forces. Some of the generals urged that they should be tried by courts martial, one remarking that the effect would be of twenty being hanged while the civil courts were hanging one. Foreseeing arrest, Lilburne decided that he must appeal to public opinion and Parliament while he was still free, and hastened to complete a petition published as *England's New Chains Discovered*. He was summoned to the bar, challenging the High Command forthrightly and calling for a limitation of the period during which they could hold office. This was, in effect, a demand that Fairfax, Cromwell and Ireton should be dismissed.

Meanwhile, agitation continued inside the army. Eight troopers presented a statement to Fairfax (probably written for them by Overton) criticizing his order restricting the right to petition Parliament. They claimed they were 'English soldiers engaged for the freedoms of England and not outlandish mercenaries to butcher the people for pay'. They remarked that the officer was nothing without 'the soldier that endureth the heat and burden of the day and performeth that work whereof the officers bear the glory and name'. They ended by declaring their agreement with Lilburne's *England's New Chains Discovered*. Fairfax was outraged. The troopers were immediately arrested; three apologized, but the remaining five were humiliatingly punished. They were told they deserved death for breeding mutiny, but 'in mercy' were cashiered after riding 'at the head of their regiments with their faces towards the horses' tails, their faults written upon their breasts and their swords broken over their heads'. Led from the parade ground, they found coaches awaiting them, which carried them off to one of the Leveller taverns, where they were entertained to a 'plentiful dinner' as the party's guests of honour.

There were soldiers who took unusual militant action. Troopers appeared in the market-place of Hitchin, fixed Lilburne's pamphlet to posts, read it aloud, and made speeches urging the people to withhold taxes and advising them not to denude themselves by giving free quarters to soldiers. 'They told the people they will live and die with them in their deliverance from such like slaveries and from this new tyranny, naming the most eminent of the army to the people.' Brailsford writes that this startling scene in Hitchin's market-place may have been repeated elsewhere, but gives no evidence. Lilburne became still more aggressive. He joined with the troops at Hitchin in urging the non-payment of taxes (perhaps he invited the soldiers to do so), and sent out propagandists to Hertfordshire, Berkshire and Hampshire to advocate the new line in the Leveller programme. The money derived from the bishops' lands, compositions, confiscated woods, parks and forests ought to be enough 'without...the cruel racking and extorting from the poor their livelihood'. A

Royalist paper commented that the poor were in revolt, if so far only here and there.

The Levellers by now had broken entirely from Cromwell and his supporters. They were mounting in membership, Lilburne boasting that for every adherent a year before they now had hundreds. They continued to print pamphlets on their underground presses – 'printed in a corner of freedom right opposite to the council of war' – and both civilians and soldiers were ready to defy flogging for distributing them. In *The Hunting of the Foxes. . . by Five Small Beagles* Overton defended the Hitchin market-place troopers (the beagles) and ridiculed the generals (the foxes). It was reasonable, he said, to require abstention in the army from politics, but it was class discrimination for generals to require it from the ranks while exercising political intervention themselves. There was a scathingly outspoken passage about the generals and Cromwell himself.

> Was there ever Overton asked a generation of men so apostate, so false and so perjured as these? Did ever men pretend an higher degree of holiness, religion and zeal to God and their country than these? These preach, these fast, these pray, these have nothing more frequent than the sentences of sacred scripture, the name of God and of Christ in their mouths. You shall scarce speak to Cromwell about anything, but he will lay his hand on his breast, elevate his eyes and call God to record, he will weep, howl and repent, even while he doth smite you under the fifth rib.

Lilburne wrote *The Second Part of England's New Chains Discovered* at much the same time. Like Overton, he concentrated on the growing power of the military leaders. He traced particularly the record of Cromwell and his deviations, and concluded that he and his senior officer associates were opportunists aiming at power and domination for themselves; they were making the army into a subservient tool and commanding the state. The House of Commons had become 'the channel through which is conveyed all the decrees and determinations of a private council of officers'. He admitted that there were some members who would be loyal to their trust; if they should fail, he was confident that the people and a 'considerable number of the soldiers' would respond to the Levellers' appeal to defeat militarism and establish a real democracy.

Cromwell hit back quickly. He ignored Overton's pamphlet, though it was the more devastating, and called on Parliament to act against Lilburne, recognizing that he was the leader who swayed the people and the troops. The Commons debate lasted three hours, Cromwell speaking, and at the end a resolution was carried that 'the authors, contrivers and framers' of *The Second Part of England's New Chains Discovered* were guilty of high treason 'and shall be processed against as traitors'. Additionally, all persons who 'shall join with and adhere unto and hereafter voluntarily aid or assist them . . . shall be esteemed as traitors to the Commonwealth and be proceeded against accordingly'. In effect, Parliament passed a sentence of death on Lilburne and his colleagues – treason was a capital offence – and threatened the whole Leveller party, if it continued with its activities, with the same charge of treason.

On the morning of 28 March 1649, between 4 and 6 a.m., four detachments of horse and foot marched to the houses respectively of Lilburne, Overton, Walwyn and Thomas Prince (treasurer of the Leveller party), and arrested and escorted them in military order through the silent streets. When his formidable escort reached St Paul's, Lilburne invited the three officers in charge of the detachment to a neighbouring tavern where the commanding officer agreed to leave his army in the City while he discreetly escorted his prisoner to Whitehall. Overton was not so lucky. He lived in crowded lodgings in Aldersgate and the officer in charge decided it was a bawdy-house. He insulted several of the women in it and arrested for fornication a trooper who was in bed with his wife. At last, with 200 horse and foot to guard him, Overton was marched through the City and the Strand to Whitehall. That evening the four prisoners were called in one by one for examination by the Council of State. Each was asked if he were an author of the offending pamphlet; each refused to answer in accordance with the Leveller principle against self-incrimination.

The prisoners were given a fair opportunity to speak, Lilburne waxing sarcastic. What sort of monster was he that 200 cavalry and infantry were required to arrest him? He congratulated the victors of a hundred battles on their conquest of four unarmed men. He understood, of course, that these forces and the choice of an early hour were a tribute to the popularity of the Levellers and a precaution against rescue. Then he became serious, arguing again the Leveller principle that legislative and judicial powers should be separated, that the Council of State was wrong to act as a court of justice which could condemn for treason. Overton was constructive as ever, proposing that the Levellers and the army should make one more effort to reach accord by reconciling their two views of *The Agreement of the People*. Walwyn, who had not attended party meetings for some months, and Prince, the treasurer, had no responsibility for the pamphlet and did not attempt to make speeches. The more fair-minded of the council were impressed. The proceedings ended with the chairman, Bradshaw, saying that the council did not propose to act as a court to try the prisoners. Lilburne's point had got through.

While they sat in an anteroom, the council debated what action to take. Lilburne laid his head to the door and swore that he heard Cromwell banging the table and exclaiming that 'I tell you, Sir, you have no other way to deal with these men, but to break them in pieces'. The heated discussion went on until after midnight. In contrast with the circumstances of their arrest, the four prisoners were allowed to go home on bail. The next day, however, they were taken to the Tower to await trial. At first they were apprehensive, both Overton and Lilburne contemplating death. Overton wrote that he would rather die in the just vindication of the cause of the oppressed people than die in his bed. Lilburne claimed to be jubilant, saying that since his conversion twelve years ago he had always felt able to lay down his life at a quarter of an hour's warning, and now, 'clothed with the glorious righteousness of Jesus Christ', he would 'sing and be merry'. It was not like the Levellers to be subjectively idle. They were accustomed to detention in the Tower, and within a few hours, Lilburne, Walwyn and Overton were writing pamphlets, enough sympathizers being present among the guards to smuggle them out. Lilburne's *The Picture of the Council of State* was a vivid description of his experiences. Walwyn's *A Manifestation* was one of the most dignified and level-headed statements of the Leveller position. It says much for the efficiency of the Levellers' underground press and for the ineffectiveness of the censorship that Lilburne's pamphlet was printed and in distribution thirteen days after he was taken to the Tower. It had an immense effect. Public sympathy can usually be aroused for victims of the powerful.

The response of the people was immediate. Within four days, 'eighty gentleman' presented themselves at the House of Commons to deliver a petition signed by 10,000 Londoners asking for a fair trial. A week later, citizens of Westminster presented a petition which showed that the stand of the prisoners was understood. Their crime, it said, was to endeavour to 'reduce the military power to a real subordination to the civil authority'. There was a succession of petitions from Southwark, from Essex, from a group of apprentices and others, but the most impressive was a demonstration at the House of Commons on 23 April by several hundred women. They were concerned that the fate of the four Levellers might become the fate of others. 'We cannot eat, drink, or sleep in peace through fear for the safety of our sons and husbands.' They wrote, too, of their distress because famine was allegedly causing several deaths every week in London, and concluded by entreating Parliament to favour *The Agreement of the People*.

Twenty women were allowed into the lobby. A member

told them to go home and wash dishes. 'Sir,' replied their leader, 'we have scarce any dishes left to wash.' Cromwell passed through the lobby and assured the women that there would be 'law' for the prisoners. 'Sir,' was the response, 'we will have your life if you take away theirs.' Finally the Serjeant-at-Arms came out to deliver a message from the Speaker. It told the women that the subject of their petition was beyond their understanding, of their folly, and that they should go home and meddle with their housewifery. There was some relief, however, when it was learned that the Speaker had assured their husbands that Lilburne and his colleagues would be tried before the King's Bench.

By their own attitude and the pressure of public opinion, the Levellers had secured a fair trial before a jury, but a strange reaction occurred both among their previous allies and their opponents. A considerable section of Baptists were alienated by their attacks on Cromwell and the Parliament of 'the Saints', declining to read Lilburne's pamphlet from their pulpits and even repudiating it in a statement to the Commons. At the same time, many of the Royalists welcomed the Levellers' conflict with Parliament and actually praised 'honest John'. A leading Royalist paper paid tribute to the prisoners for their 'interest in freedom against the present tyranny' and expressed the conviction that experience would teach them that 'a just monarch is the best guardian of public liberty'. These two reactions were warnings for the future. The Levellers still hoped that Cromwell would accept Overton's suggestion of reconciliation on the *Agreement of the People*; they would give up other demands if Cromwell and his supporters would accept a version nearer to their original draft than Ireton's document.

In this they failed to recognize the fundamental diversion of Cromwell's basic political philosophy. Cromwell was not a liberal. He was opposed to religious toleration for Catholics and atheists, and was against democracy in the army, favouring a disciplined national force. There was an even deeper divergence. The Levellers stood for a decentralized state with the least government at the centre. Cromwell stood for a strong centralized state which he believed was the only means of imposing a solution of existing divisions and discontents within society and of establishing Britain as a power among nations. He was dedicated not only to restoring the occupation of Ireland, but also to extending British influence overseas, an early dream of Empire. Between these two conceptions there could be no agreement.

The conflict in Ireland brought these differences to a head. The Levellers were magnificently forthright in their opposition to the reconquest of Ireland, pioneers against imperialism as they were in many spheres. They published their customary pamphlets, demonstrated, and did not hesitate to campaign in the army. Cromwell, appointed by Parliament to lead the invading force, did not scruple to win adherence by concessions to those troops who were willing to go and by penalization of those who refused. Food and clothing were distributed among the consenting men, Parliament voted them three months' arrears of pay; those who refused to go were cashiered and sent home with barely enough cash to pay for the journey. One colonel stripped them of their coats before dispatching them. In spite of this treatment, 300 soldiers of his regiment laid down their arms. The Levellers watched with horror as the New Model Army was turned into a mercenary professional force.

Lilburne and his colleagues, particularly the near-pacifist Walwyn, taught a new conception of international morality – 'a startling advance in civilization', writes Brailsford. They saw in the Catholic Irish their fellow men whose claim to liberty was as valid as their own. Their pamphlet, *The English Soldier's Standard*, almost certainly written by Walwyn, said bluntly, 'It will be no satisfaction to God's justice to plead that you murdered men in obedience to your generals.' A persuasive paragraph followed, reminding them of the wrongs they suffered in England:

For consider, as things now stand, to what end you should

hazard your lives against the Irish. Will you go on still to
kill, slay and murder in order to make them your officers
as absolute lords and masters over Ireland as you have made
them over England? Or is it your ambition to reduce the
Irish to the happiness of tithes upon treble damages, to
excise, customs and monopolies in trade? Or to fill their
prisons with poor, disabled persons, to fill their land with
swarms of beggars, . . . to take down monarchical tyranny
and set up an aristocratic tyranny?

The pamphlet appealed to the troops to remedy the evils
here before going to Ireland, and to insist on the
reconstitution of a representative Assembly of the Army
elected from every regiment.

A second pamphlet addressed to the troops was more
fundamental, calling on them to answer in their consciences
eighteen probing questions. The soldiers were asked:

Whether the land or inheritance that any nation hath for so
many hundreds of years enjoyed . . . be not their right which
God and nature has given them . . . How can the conquered
be accounted rebels, if at any time they seek to free themselves and recover their own . . . Whether it be not the duty
of every honest man to divert, what he can, the intended
expedition? . . . Whether it be not England's duty to repent
of the oppressions and usurpations over the Irish nation by
their kings and forefathers.

The sixteenth question was long but it expressed the Levellers' alternative to the military suppression of the Irish rebellion:

Whether if the state of England, now in their full strength,
should send and proclaim Ireland a free state, repenting of
all the evil themselves have acted and intended, and that
our kings have formerly acted against that nation, and that
they will not further act to their prejudice; but only sit down

by them as a neighbour state, as Holland doth: desire only to be in mutual league as friends, to seek the peace and welfare of each other, not countenance or assist to protect each other's enemies, nor any that shall disturb the peace of nations, only require some considerable seaports or towns for security and bond to tie the Irish to performance of covenants, whether this may not be every way as advantageous to the state and people of England as a conquest of them, the charge considered?

It is a little doubtful whether the Irish would have accepted the designation of seaports or towns as securities, but, that apart, the publication of these pamphlets represented a crisis for the Levellers. They were an act of ultimate defiance. The Levellers had become rebels.

Meanwhile, things were happening in the army. A local dispute over pay brought tragedy. When troops billeted at the Bull Inn at Bishopsgate were ordered to move to Essex, they refused to stir until they received some of their arrears since they had to pay for their quarters. Thirty of the men seized the Colours and took up armed positions in the gallery of the inn. They yielded only when Fairfax and Cromwell arrived. The court martial sentenced six troopers to death and five to be cashiered after humiliation. On Cromwell's intercession, those sentenced to death were reprieved, with one significant exception, Robert Lockyer. Lockyer was a courageous Leveller, a leader in the army intransigence in 1647. He was only twenty-three years old, though he had served seven years. He was of fine character and much beloved. Lilburne and Overton hastily improvised a petition, but in vain. Refusing to wear a bandage over his eyes, he was shot to death in front of St Paul's. On the following Sunday, the funeral indicated the sympathy he had in the army. Six trumpeters headed the procession sounding the last post, followed by hundreds of troopers on horse and infantry. Then, though he was a common trooper, his horse, draped in black, was led by associates in mourning cloaks, an honour usually reserved for high commanders. On his coffin, borne by six soldiers, his naked sword lay upon sprigs of rosemary dipped in his blood; his kinsmen followed, and after them many hundreds of citizens concluding with a contingent of women. Everyone wore ribbons of the Leveller sea-green, and also ones of black. A current report said that thousands awaited the coffin at the grave. Robert Lockyer became a Leveller martyr.

Lord Hale (colleague of the author in the Commons and Africa) found in Thomas Carlyle's edition of *Oliver Cromwell's Letters and Speeches* a section devoted to the Levellers which had detailed descriptions of important incidents. They were written by Lord (Sir) Bulstrode Whitelocke, a close associate of Cromwell, Ambassador to Sweden, a member of the Council of State, Keeper of the Seal, who apparently chronicled these events for the Lord Protector. His impressions are important in confirming the accounts which Brailsford gave; his record of the Bull mutiny is worth quoting fully, not only because it endorses Brailsford but for its tribute to Trooper Lockyer. Heading his note 'Monday 26th April', Lord Whitelocke wrote:

> The General and the Lieutenant-General have to hasten thither; quell them, pack them forth on their march; seizing fifteen of them first, to be tried by court-martial. Tried by instant court-martial, five of them are found guilty, doomed to die, but pardoned; and one of them, Trooper Lockyer, is shot, in Paul's churchyard, on the morrow. A very brave young man, they say, though but three and twenty, he has served seven years in the Wars, ever since the War began. Religious, too, of excellent parts and much beloved; but with hot motives as to human Freedom and the rate at which the millenniums are attainable. Poor Lockyer! He falls shot in Paul's churchyard on Friday, amid the tears of men and women. Paul's churchyard, we remark, is now a Horseguard; horses stamp in the Canon's stalls there; and Paul's cross itself, as smacking of Popery, where in fact Alabaster once preached

flat Popery, is swept away and its leaden roof melted into bullets, or mixed with tin for culinary pewter. Lockyer's corpse is watched and wept over, not without prayer: and on Monday, this is what we see advancing westward by way of funeral to him.

The irrepressible Levellers issued another appeal to the army, this time only a single-sheet leaflet, distributed in thousands. It called on the troops to 'keep every man in his place and post and stir not, but immediately choose you out a Council of Agitators once more'. It must not be thought that this was a campaign imposed on the army from outside. The leaflets had to be printed and published by civilians, but there was a spontaneous uprising within the forces. This was dramatically and tragically demonstrated. In the spring of 1649, four regiments of horse and two of foot elected Agitators. When a regiment was ordered to march westward to embark for Ireland, it refused to proceed beyond Salisbury, which it reached on May Day. The troops mutinied. In a letter to the Speaker of the Commons, recorded by Henry Cary in his *Memorials of the Great Civil War in England*, General Fairfax wrote 'those troops at Salisbury, of Colonel Scroope's regiment, did wholly reject their officers, except one lieutenant and two or three junior ones'. While the production of protests had to be by civilians, one was written by a soldier, probably among those who stopped marching at Salisbury.

'What have we to do in Ireland he asked , to fight and murder a people and nation (for indeed they the High Command are set upon cruelty and murdering poor people, which is all they glory in) which have done us no harm . . . ? We have waded too far in that crimson stream already of innocent and Christian blood.'

The mutinous troops at Salisbury did not stand still. It would be wrong to suggest that they all refused to proceed to Ireland. Most were ready to go if grievances could be met, particularly the deprivation of arrears payments to those who did not choose to serve overseas. They put this well in a resolution: 'It is as if a man should owe a servant £20, and then tell him he will give them £5 of the same, upon condition that he will do another service for him (which is greater) in another place.' There was a surprising sequence. When the officers realized that the men would no longer obey orders, eighty of them, including the colonel in charge, quitted the regiment. The men elected officers to replace them, and 'with joy and acclamation' adopted a declaration prepared by their Agitators, repeating the call for a general council of two officers and two men chosen by each regiment, together with the High Command. This council they would obey. When news came that Fairfax and Cromwell were preparing to march against them, they issued an appeal to their 'dear fellow soldiers' not to draw their swords against them.

Simultaneously, a group of 300 Leveller supporters from three regiments as well as civilians from London assembled at Oxford under the leadership of an unusual character, William Thompson, a corporal but self-styled captain. His physical courage was legendary. The army heads described him as hot-tempered, much too quick with the sword, but Lilburne trusted him and cooperated. At Banbury, on the way to Oxford, Thompson issued a spirited manifesto. The cries and groans of the poor, he wrote (or was Lilburne the author?), the breaking in of beggary and famine like a mighty torrent, the barbarous taxes, the setting up of bloody and tyrannical courts – these things, as well as the dissolution of the Council of Agitators and the iniquities of martial law, had forced action. If a hair of the heads of the four Leveller prisoners in the Tower were touched, he and his men would avenge it seventy times sevenfold. The manifesto concluded by a declaration of solidarity with the mutineers at Salisbury. The determination of those who gathered at Oxford was not, however, as spirited as the manifesto. When a near-by colonel marched on them, the majority surrendered, the rest dispersing. As Thompson rode off, he was pursued. Turning, he shot dead one officer, wounded another, dismounted a third and made good his escape with a handful of partisans.

Fairfax and Cromwell summoned the force mobilized to suppress the Salisbury mutiny to a review in Hyde Park. It is reported that many of the men, even in the selected crack regiments of horse, wore the sea-green ribbons of the Levellers in their hats. The commanders were well aware of the wide disquiet in the army, and Cromwell made a conciliatory speech, giving two promises which met to a considerable degree the main demands of the discontented. First, he said, 'those who thought martial law to be a burden should have liberty to lay down their arms and receive tickets for the payment of their arrears, which should as punctually be discharged as the arrears of those that stayed'. Secondly, he gave a pledge that the officers' version of *The Agreement of the People* would be carried out, including 'putting a period to this present Parliament'. These were important concessions, but the officers' draft of *The Agreement* did not satisfy the Levellers – and the invasion of Ireland was to proceed. Indeed, Fairfax emphasized this in a declaration to the mutineers made after Cromwell's speech. He told them they would be defying God if they disobeyed His clear call for service in Ireland. 'If you submit,' he concluded, 'I am ready and willing to pass by and pardon.' Otherwise, 'I shall endeavour by force to reduce you.'

Meanwhile, the Salisbury mutineers had marched to Abingdon with the aim of linking up with a horse regiment from Buckinghamshire before advancing west to link up with resisting troopers in Gloucester. Fairfax and Cromwell planned to cut them off before the four regiments got together, and, to delay action, sent messengers led by Major White to negotiate. The choice of White was wise. He was one of the few senior officers the men trusted, having taken their part in the revolt of 1647. Fairfax and Cromwell appeared still to be in a conciliatory mood, telling White that the object was to end division in the army and assuring him that it was not their intention to follow the negotiating messengers by force. The Levellers in the Salisbury regiment doubted his assurance, but White avowed that if the forces of the generals should fall upon them he would stand between them and the bullets.

The scepticism of the Levellers proved right. On their way to Gloucester the Salisbury troopers were billeted in the village of Burford. During that day, 14 May, Cromwell, with 2,000 cavalry and dragoons, covered forty-five miles, and at midnight fell upon Burford, subduing the mutineers with scarcely a fired shot. Major White was as good as his word. When he heard of the presence of Cromwell he rushed out in his slippers to find him, only to be taken prisoner. Three hundred and forty of the mutineers were placed under guard in the church. Some 500 escaped, but without their horses, which fell as booty to the Royalists. Leaderless, these men never rallied, making their way embittered to their homes. Four of the prisoners were selected for trial by court martial, and three were shot in the presence of their fellows. Cromwell's victory over the mutineers and their Leveller supporters was complete, but there still rings in many ears the blunt verdict of these too credulous troopers: 'You kept not covenant with us.'

We quote again from Lord Whitelocke, Cromwell's colleague. In Carlyle's book, a description is given by him of the executions in the churchyard at Burford. Whitelocke stated that Cornet Thompson, brother of the leader of the mutiny, acknowledged his execution was just, and continued:

Next after him was a Corporal, brought to the same place of execution, where, looking upon his fellow mutineers, he set his back against the wall; and bade them who were appointed to shoot 'Shoot' and died desperately. The third, being also a Corporal, was brought to the same place; and without the least acknowledgement of error, or show of fear, he pulled off his doublet, standing a pretty distance from the wall; and bade the soldiers do their duty; looking them in the face till they gave fire, not showing the least kind of terror or fearfulness of spirit.

Carlyle's own comment is of historic interest.

So die the Leveller Corporals he wrote , strong they, after their sort, for the Liberties of England; resolute to the very death, Misguided Corporals! But History which has wept for a misguided Charles Stuart, and blubbered, in the most copious hapless manner, near two centuries now, whole floods of brine, enough to salt the Herring-fishery — will not refuse these poor Corporals also her tributary sigh. With Arnold of the Rendezvous of Ware, with Lockyer of the Bull in Bishopsgate, and other mis-guided martyrs to the Liberties of England, then and since, may they sleep well!

It is time to return to the four prisoners in the Tower, Lilburne, Overton, Walwyn and Prince, still awaiting trial. They spent their time preparing a final draft of *The Agreement of the People*, which they preceded by a repudiation of the charges commonly levelled against them. They were not atheists, Jesuits, Royalists or communists. Today what they wrote about the last charge is of most interest, but it must be borne in mind that communism in the seventeenth century was different from the modern conception which emerged from the World War of 1914 to 1918. In the context of the essentially religious consciousness of the seventeenth century, communism meant the egalitar-ianism of the first Christians, the sharing of all things in common. Lilburne and his followers rejected this egalitarianism, and many of their arguments to rebut the charge of communism are curiously similar to those used against Marxists today. Lilburne was the most rigid individualist of the three Leveller leaders. This is what he wrote about communism in a reference to the Diggers:

In my opinion and judgment this conceit of levelling propriety and magistracy is so ridiculous and foolish an opinion as no man of brains, reason or ingenuity can be imagined such a sot as to maintain such a principle, because it would, if practised, destroy not only any industry in the world, but raze the very foundation of generation and of subsistence . . . As for industry and valour, by which the societies of mankind are maintained and preserved, who will take pains for that which when he has gotten it is not his own but must equally be shared in by every lazy, simple, droning sot?

However, Walwyn, who wrote the preface to this final edition of *The Agreement*, was a convinced egalitarian, favouring equality in education and advocating a near approach to equality of income. Given the duty of rebutting communism, he avoided the issue by merely saying that it was not in the party programme.

There is no doubt that the third edition of *The Agreement* was the most historically significant document to which the Leveller leaders put their signatures. Amazingly, the four prisoners — Lilburne, Overton, Walwyn and Prince — revised their long and detailed statement in two weeks. It has sometimes been referred to as the Levellers' programme. It was not that. Their programme of reforms is to be found in the series of demands they presented to Parliament, which are listed in the *Conclusions* to this book (pages 146 − 7). The purpose of *The Agreement* was to present a proposal which would unite all diverse democratic elements, 'Tendered as a peace-offering to this distressed Nation', accompanied by Matthew 5, verse 9, 'Blessed are the Peace-makers, for they shall be called the children of God.' It was an effort to produce an agreed consensus rather than a partisan manifesto, with the consequence that many of the Levellers' demands regarded as extreme were omitted. Above everything, *The Agreement* was intended to be a broad statement of fundamental rights to express 'the sovereignty of the people', *more authoritative than any decisions in Parliament through terms of reference which could never be disobeyed by a legislature*. This revolutionary idea was an extraordinary anticipation of the proposal in the 1970s for a Bill of Rights which Parliament would not be allowed to repudiate in legislation or administration.

One must acknowledge that the precedent which the Levellers proposed indicates the dangers as well as the advantages of the proposal. *The Agreement of the People* included some romantic ideas which, however relevant to immediate circumstances, did not stand the challenge of continuing events. Nevertheless, much was permanent and recognition should be accorded to the Leveller leaders for pioneering so many principles of democracy which have since been accepted. Lilburne, Overton, Walwyn and Prince deserve a much greater place in history than they have been given.

The full text of *The Agreement of the People* has been given in Wolfe's *Leveller Manifestoes of the Puritan Revolution* and in Aylmer's *The Levellers in the English Revolution*. Many will wish to read the full text for an incidental interest.

Readers must already have been intrigued by the terminology of Leveller and parliamentary documents, their Shakespearian turn of phrase and religious preoccupation. *The Agreement of the People* provides uniquely an opportunity to flavour the captivating quality of seventeenth-century writings. Here, however, we must be content to state in modern terms the main proposals of the thirty articles of *The Agreement* in the following summary.

The Electorate

Manhood suffrage, with the exclusion of (1) servants (2) those receiving alms, (3) Royalists who fought with the King or voluntarily supported him (disqualified for ten years).

All property qualifications ended.

Rotten boroughs abolished.

The Central Government

Long Parliament to be dissolved, August 1649.
Parliaments to sit for one year.

Four hundred members.
No member eligible for re-election.
No salaried officer or revenue official eligible.
No elected lawyer to practise in courts.
Abolition of Council of State.
Government by representative committees.

Legislative Reservations

(The following required by any succeeding Parliament)

Toleration of all religions and of none.
No State Church.
Abolition of tithes (with compensation).
No compulsion to contribute towards maintenance of a
    minister of religion.
Each parish to elect its minister.
Alternative places of worship permitted.
Catholics not eligible for public office.
Abolition of 'pressing' or conscription for military service.
Amnesty for all belligerent acts in civil war.

Civil Rights

All equal before the law.
No martial law in peace-time.
No compulsory billeting in peace-time.

Judicial Principles

No one to be condemned 'where no law before provided'.
Parliament to have no function as court of law.
No one under arrest to be required to incriminate himself.
No extortion of confessions.
All proceedings in law to be terminated in six months.
Prisoners permitted to plead own case or choose another to
    do so (not necessarily a lawyer).
No imprisonment for debt.
Personal estates liable for repayment of debts.
Capital punishment abolished, except for murder, heinous

offences destructive of society and attempts by force to destroy this Agreement.

Revision of entire scale of punishments.

No estate to be confiscated for a trivial offence.

Decentralization

All trials to be by twelve men of the neighbourhood chosen by the people.

All central Courts, including Chancery, King's Bench, and Privy Council, to be abolished.

Practice of centrally appointed judges on circuit ended.

People to elect all officers administering the law, including sheriffs and justices of the peace 'for one whole year and no longer'.

Defence

Parliament (1) to decide total force and character of service, (2) to appoint commanding general and senior officers at centre, and (3) to assign to each county, town or borough the number of men to be enlisted, equipped and payed.

Electors to choose officers of local forces and have power to remove them.

Economics

Abolition of all monopolies in foreign trade (e.g. the Merchant Adventurers and East India Company).

All indirect taxation on commodities to be ended within four months.

Revenue to be raised 'only by an equal rate in the pound for every real and personal estate'.

Abolition of customs except for power to forbid certain imports and exports.

To modern minds, this must seem an extraordinary statement of fundamental rights, but it reflected the controversies of the time. Its underlying principle was participating democracy, reduced power of a remote Parliament and direct local control of justice, Church and army. Personal liberties denied in the seventeenth century were emphasized: religious liberty, liberty before the law, liberty from military conscription. Equality was stressed: equality before the law, equality in taxation – the remarkable insistence, for the first time, on direct taxation proportionate to income. Noteworthy, too, is the earliest proposal for the separation of the legislature and the judiciary, and the abolition, with some reservations (one startling) of the death penalty. To those of British experience, the election of public officials will seem unrealistic until one remembers that it is done in the United States. When seats in Parliament depended on the wealth or patronage at an M.P.'s disposal, the proposals for the democratization of the electorate were revolutionary. The abolition of the 'rotten boroughs' and of property qualifications, and the introduction of manhood suffrage (still too early, alas, for women). The one proposal reactionary in principle was the exclusion of Catholics from eligibility for public office. This was contrary to all Leveller campaigning for religious tolerance, a disappointing concession to the public opinion required for *The Agreement of the People*.

Professor Macpherson, in his *Political Theory of Positive Individualism*, has denied that the Levellers stood for manhood suffrage, arguing that their reservations would have disfranchised all wage-earners. This was certainly not the intention of the Levellers and an analysis of the population would seem to show that under their proposals well over three quarters of the male populace would actually have been entitled to vote. The difficulty is the definition of 'servants'. It would have applied to employees of a single master, admittedly more frequent than now, his domestics and perhaps to his fully employed estate labourers, but these were only a minority of wage-earners, many of whom were employed by companies, while others were rural workers, often casually employed, or members of peasant families farming small plots of land. In addition to these wage-earners, the men in the armed forces and the many small tradesmen and independent craftsmen would be enfranchised. The purpose of the Levellers in making the reservation of servants was to avoid intimidation at the hustings (there was no secret ballot). It was not likely that the general body of wage-earners would be intimidated, but the 'servants' of single employers would certainly have feared to vote by publicly lifting hands against the wishes of the lord and master on whom their livelihoods depended.

The Agreement of the People was accompanied by a list of immediate reforms additional to those in the main text. This approached a programme, but even here some of the more militant demands which the Levellers had made were not mentioned, doubtless to save prejudicing supporters. Nevertheless the proposals attached to *The Agreement* were comprehensive. They included in summary:

The provision at public expense in every county of hospitals for the 'nurture, maintenance or relief' of the sick, the lame, orphans, widows and the aged.

Free primary education for all (certainly for boys).

Agrarian reform, including the conversion of base tenures (with obligations to the landlord) into freeholds, the restoration to the poor of their enclosures, and the utilization of wasteland; the election by the poor of a trustee or 'tribune of the people' to recover lost endowments or common land; and a land register in every county to record all bills, bonds and the like.

The limitation of interest to 6 per cent.

Freedom of the press, including the printing and distribution of publications.

Prison reform – the gaoler (who ran the prison for profit) becoming a public servant.

The codification of civil and criminal law.

It is worth adding that the only items in this list in fact enacted by the Long Parliament were the limitation of interest, the setting up of a land register, and an emasculated and ineffective version of the proposal to forbid imprisonment for debt.

At this point, there came an attack on the Levellers from an unexpected source. With the support of Parliament, a pamphlet was licensed over the names of the seven leading Nonconformist divines, both Baptist and Congregationalist, attacking William Walwyn for his *English Soldiers' Standard*, alleging that he was a Jesuit who misled his 'simple-hearted and simple-headed companions'. The title sufficiently indicated its tone: *Walwyn's Wiles or the Manifestators Manifested...Declaring the Subtle and Crafty Wiles, the Atheistical, Blasphemous, Soul-murdering Principles and Practices of Mr William Walwyn*. The dissident churches might be in favour of religious tolerance for themselves, but they were at this moment even more in favour of war against the Papists in Ireland. In the eyes of the authors of this pamphlet, however, the chief crime of the Levellers was that they fomented class war and (Walwyn in particular) advocated equality. The significance of this attack was that it confirmed the breach between what had been regarded as the Puritan 'left' and the Levellers. In the pulpits of the dissident churches, Lilburne and his associates were denounced as strongly as in the Presbyterian churches. The political effect was considerable because 'the Saints' in Parliament were to a large extent subordinate to the religious leaders. They claimed to be acting for God and they took the advice of the voices of God.

The Levellers became increasingly isolated. They were concerned with democracy at the grass roots, and for justice to the poor, and they began to recognize that both could be violated as much under a dictatorial Parliament as under a monarchy. Said Lilburne, 'I had rather by many degrees choose to live under a regulated and well-bounded King without tyranny than under any government with tyranny.' Opposition to the Rump Parliament deepened when it passed the Treason Act, transferring the capital crime from war against the King (of which most of them had been guilty) to opinion calculated to undermine the prestige and authority of the party in power. Parliament declared that it was high treason (to quote Brailsford's summary), 'Maliciously to affirm the present government to be tyrannical, usurped or unlawful; or that the Commons in Parliament are not the supreme authority; or to endeavour to alter the government. Or to affirm the Parliament or Council of State to be tyrannical or unlawful, or to endeavour to subvert them or stir up sedition against them. Or for any person to stir up mutiny in the army.' Under this definition of treason, the Levellers were guilty. They declared that Parliament was tyrannical, they claimed that the people were the supreme authority; their leaders were in prison on the charge of stirring mutiny in the army.

For a time Leveller leaders became depressed. They were themselves in prison. Their supporters in the army had been defeated at Burford. Their Puritan allies had deserted them. Parliament had taken final powers to suppress them. Overton wrote to their followers at the Whalebone Tavern of the 'dumps' into which the imprisoned leaders had fallen, but nevertheless beseeching their followers outside prison to renewed activity on behalf of 'our persecuted, wounded, forsaken and almost murdered Cause'. A personal tragedy reduced Lilburne to inaction. His family fell victims to smallpox, his two sons died and his wife and daughter only just escaped with their lives. He had one compensation. In prison news reached him that his elder son was praying for a sight of his father before he died. Parliament showed some humanity. On the motion of Henry Marten, Lilburne was released from prison during daylight. But the effect of these losses on him was profound. He lost the will to fight. He longed for a 'composure' with his adversaries. He cancelled the publication of a pamphlet in the printer's hands; he was even on the point of burning it. The leaderless Levellers were in a bad way.

Meanwhile, Parliament was seeking to come to terms with

its expelled Presbyterians, still powerful because theirs was the State Church with its influential pulpit propaganda. The 'Rump' promised that their tithes would not be taken away until a way to maintain their ministers, no less large and honourable, was found. In return, Parliament asked that ministers should refrain from meddling in affairs of state, and even carried a Bill which forbade them, directly or indirectly, to preach or pray publicly against the power, authority or proceedings of the present Parliament. The measure went too far to win the acquiescence of many in the powerful Puritan group who desired conciliation with the Presbyterians, Cromwell and Ireton voting against it, but political circumstances favoured consensus. Cromwell was now to play a less personal part in Parliament. Three days later he left to take command in Ireland. He drove in a magnificent coach drawn by six horses, escorted by a lifeguard of eighty troopers, all officers or esquires, wearing flaunting feathers in their hats, uniformed in dazzling white. As they approached Bristol a boy was heard to say, 'they will be dyed red enough before they return from thence'. He was apprehended and taken into custody.

Lilburne recovered and was probably more militant through remorse for his withdrawal. He defied the Treason Act by an audacious counter-attack, accusing the High Command of treason. His pamphlet, *An Impeachment of High Treason against Oliver Cromwell and his son-in-law Henry Ireton*, addressed in warm comradely language to followers at the Whalebone Tavern, revived hope among the militants, despite the fact that the printing press was discovered and broken into pieces. Lilburne alleged that Cromwell meant to make himself king and appealed for a national conference to take a decision to support no one, neither 'the present men in power' nor Prince Charles, who declined to accept the principles of *The Agreement of the People*. He went to the extreme point of suggesting that Prince Charles might be better as king than the 'pretended false Saint Oliver'. While he insisted that the prince must not be restored 'by conquest by the hands of foreigners', he argued that, because of his good relations with foreign powers, peace might be made secure and all armies and garrisons (save the defensive Cinque Ports) be disbanded. On the other hand, there would under Cromwell be 'wars and the cutting of throats year after year; yea and the absolute keeping up of a perpetual and everlasting Army, under which the people are absolute and perfect slaves and vassals . . . And therefore rouse up your spirits before it be too late to a vigorous promotion of the aforesaid *Agreement*.'

Lilburne succeeded in revitalizing the spirits of the party. Six troopers published *The Levellers Vindicated*, appealing to every regiment to appoint delegates to the proposed national conference; and ten representatives of City apprentices issued another outspoken pamphlet, *An Outcry of the Young Men and Apprentices of London*, urging every ward to nominate delegates. The latter pamphlet, in which Lilburne's hand is clearly revealed, was significant because it advanced still further conditional support for Prince Charles, even arguing that the execution of his father was illegal, since Parliament had no mandate from the people who had engaged in the civil war to destroy kingship but only to regulate it.

One actual instance of mutiny occurred in the army. In September 1649 a foot regiment at Oxford insisted on electing agents (the term Agitators being dropped) who demanded the restoration of regimental representatives in the Army Council as well as a large payment of arrears. Repulsed, they seized officers and imprisoned them in New College. When the mutineers claimed that thousands of fellow-soldiers from neighbouring counties would join them the command in London took alarm and dispatched a regiment of horse and dragoons to suppress them; before they arrived the local major and five of his officers succeeded in releasing the colonel and his fellow prisoners and in arresting all the men's agents. A court martial sentenced three of the mutineers to death (one was pardoned) and six to the barbarous ordeal of running the gauntlet (beaten between two rows of strikers). Six sympathetic officers were cashiered.

Military unrest turned to industrial unrest. Four thousand lead miners in Derbyshire revolted against the Earl of Rutland, who would not permit them to dig for ore in the neighbourhood of his house. The miners urged that he was putting his single interest against the interests of the nation and offered to submit their case to the arbitration of the court of the Duchy of Cornwall, which had jurisdiction not only in its own tin-mining county but in mining of tin and lead throughout England. The Rump Parliament, always eager to enhance its own authority as a court of law, insisted, however, on keeping the matter in its own hands, and in due course its committee found against the miners.

The reaction was fierce. On the pretext of attending a sporting match, 5,000 miners gathered in a rebellious mood, half of them on horseback, armed with pistols and swords. Parliament was prepared. It had in readiness a regiment of cavalry who fell upon the miners, seizing their horses and swords, and driving them to disperse. Once again, the forces of the state had overcome revolt, but it cost them more and more discontent. The Derbyshire miners became resolute adherents of the Levellers, from whom they had had strenuous support. They endorsed *The Agreement* and backed the proposal for a national peoples' conference.

Parliament realized that there was a dangerous revolutionary psychology in the country and it occurred to someone in the governing circle – Henry Marten? – that an effort should be made to close the rift with the Levellers before they came to terms with the Royalists. In the first week of September 1649, several meetings took place between representatives of the Commons and of the army, on the one side, and the acting officers of the Levellers on the other. The talks seem to have gone well because Parliament decided to bring in Overton, Walwyn and Prince, still confined to prison with Lilburne, who was continuing to enjoy daylight parole – not without adventure. He told how a few days earlier a file of musketeers, to the alarm of his wife, came to arrest him in his absence. When he arrived he repeated previous performances by convincing them that their warrant gave them no power to take him. Shamefaced, they departed with Leveller pamphlets in their hands and pockets! The meeting between Parliament, the army and the Levellers broke down after two days of discussion. There is no report of what happened, but Royalists said the Levellers had refused to compromise.

Parliament now took a drastic offensive. The Commons condemned the apprentices' *Outcry of the Young Men* as seditious and decreed that the 'contrivers' should be tried for high treason before an extraordinary tribunal chosen for the occasion. Everyone knew that Lilburne was in reality the sole contriver. At the same time, the Commons instructed its executive, the Council of State, to prepare a *Declaration against the Levellers* for wide distribution – the Rump had learned the value of propaganda.

A savage and fatal blow was struck at the press. Three censors were appointed, one to act for Parliament, another for the Council of State, the third for the High Command in the army, to whom the authors, publishers and printers of all books, pamphlets and newspapers were made subject. If a newspaper contained any news or opinions about Parliament, the council or the army, it must receive the *imprimatur* of all three censors. Printers were required to find two sureties of £300 that they would print nothing treasonable. The Stationers' Company was given powers to seize and break up any press which printed unlicensed matter. Any purchaser of an unlicensed publication was made liable to imprisonment, and all hawkers, mercuries (women street sellers) and balladsingers were threatened with whipping and loss of their stock if they handled illegal sheets. There were penalties for dispersing unlicensed matter by post or transport, and the manufacture of presses and type was also controlled. No printing was permitted, save in London, Oxford, Cambridge and York, where there were facilities for control. This unprecedented draconian law came into force on 1 October 1649.

Parliament was nevertheless uneasy. Except against the press, it did not dare to make use of the totalitarian measures with which it had armed itself. Month after month it put off the trial of Lilburne. It even attempted to bribe him. It was not only the Levellers and the Royalists who were defying its authority. In face of the unanimous hostility of the Presbyterian clergy, its Act for muzzling the pulpit was little more than a dead letter. In Devon and Dorset ministers of religion called a conference to organize defiance of Parliament and openly declared themselves supporters of the King, the Lords and the excluded reactionary Commoners.

The Levellers misjudged the nature of the opposition to Westminster. They published a call for revolution. Somehow the *Remonstrance of Many Thousands of the Free People of England* was printed and distributed. 'Our burdens,' the Levellers proclaimed, 'became so insupportable that we are . . . compelled to make use of that means nature teacheth us for our own preservation.' They invited disobedience to all the orders of 'the usurpers', and especially a refusal to pay all taxes and tithes. This call for massive non-cooperation was followed by a listing of the Leveller aims, more revolutionary than heretofore. They would bring to justice all who murdered their friends at Ware, London, Oxford and Burford. They would force all M.P.s to disgorge their estates over and above what they owned at the beginning of the Parliament. A new demand, perhaps thinking of the Derbyshire miners, was the right to work. They promised when victorious to refer to the counties the question of 'one head or king'. Finally there came an open call for armed action. 'For the attainment of all these ends,' the Levellers said for the first time, 'we have drawn our swords and are resolved not to put them up again till we have obtained the things before specified, not doubting of the aid and assistance of all honest and well-meaning men.'

It was claimed that 98,064 hands had signed this call for revolution, and more were promised when it was circulated 'to our afflicted brethren in all the counties of England and Wales'. If this figure was true, it was a remarkable achievement in view of the authoritarian repression of activity. Brailsford was inclined to accept it, though he thinks it likely that many who signed did not appreciate its implications and were concerned only to express their hostility to the 'usurpers'. He estimated that at this moment the Levellers in an election would have received more votes than the Cromwellian Puritans, though the Presbyterians would have headed the poll. Be that as it may, the appeal for revolution failed. The army had been purged of its militant democrats, and while urban workers and rural peasants may have been in a rebellious mood, they were not organized for revolution and, more important, were without adequate arms or the discipline of units. This was the weakness of the Leveller manifesto: propaganda without action. It was reported that the Leveller leaders were divided. It is certainly difficult to think that pacifist-inclined Walwyn agreed.

Parliament retorted by publishing its case against the Levellers, prepared by the Council of State, *A Declaration of the Parliament of England*. It adopted all the prejudices. Political arguments were included, attacking the advocacy of 'liberty without property', association with Royalists, opposition to the war in Ireland, the aim to dissolve Parliament. But also there was abuse: the Levellers were turning to 'atheism and licentiousness'. It was the concluding paragraph which alerted public attention. After referring to the army mutinies, it called for justice upon 'the chief of those who laid and avowed on these dangerous designs'. Everyone understood that the reference was to John Lilburne. He would be tried for treason, the penalty for which was death.

The threat to Lilburne had an extraordinary psychological effect. The national conference for *The Agreement of the People* was forgotten. The revolution was forgotten. Every Leveller, every supporter of the Levellers, had one concern only, to save Lilburne. This was a remarkable tribute to his personality and leadership, even if it put in a secondary place his aims. Lilburne himself responded as he always did to a personal crisis. He rushed out *Strength out of Weakness*, memorable for an epigram which has become historic: 'No man can be a slave but he that is afraid to die.' He added: 'I bless God I have already learned to die, having ever since my first contest with the bishops always carried my life in my own hand, ready at a quarter of an hour's warning to lay it down.' On 27 September Lilburne was imprisoned without parole, and on 13 October the Council of State fixed his trial before a grand jury for 24 October. His spirit rose and fell. At one moment he challenged Cromwell to submit the case against him to arbitration; the next he proposed his own banishment, offering to go to the West Indies. Had his wife Elizabeth proposed this, or his devoted brother Robert? Or was John disappointed that his aims for action had not received more support?

The trial took place in the Guildhall. Justice cannot be done to it here in the space we have available. Interested readers should buy, borrow or go to their libraries for Brailsford's book. His description is one of his finest writings. Through his words we can see the scene, the colourful robes of the judges and of the legal officials who accompanied them — 'blazing with scarlet, ermine and gold, blending with the sombre purple and black, the dais would sparkle like a bed of autumnal flowers' — and of the prisoner at the bar, 'a slight and rather elegant figure, tense and alert', he, too, in scarlet coat to remind his audience that he once commanded the dragoons at Marston Moor. As we read on we can hear the dialogue and watch what happens: Lilburne's courage and his sensitive appeal to the jury, the casual Attorney-General, sure that he would win, the dignified courtesy of the bench breaking down at times, the tense listening of the spectators, the drama of the verdict.

Lilburne was at his best in trials, as previous occasions had shown. He was uninhibited, never overawed, persistent in pressing ingenious legal points, very human, knowing how to move the jury. At the very beginning he challenged procedure. He was asked to plead. Instead, he asked to be represented by counsel and complained that the gates of the court were shut and guarded by armed men while courts should be open and accessible to all. The presiding judge gave an order to the sentries and said, 'Mr Lilburne, look behind you.' The doors were open. His third point was substantial. He argued that trial by the special tribunal was illegal as contrary to the Petition of Rights and to an Act of 1641. His fourth point was that, as his alleged offences were committed in Southwark, he should be tried in Surrey and not in the City of London. Finally, he complained that he could not read the 'illegible parchment' of his summons, writ in an unusual hand and in Latin, of which he said, not quite truthfully, he knew only a few words. The Attorney-General did not attempt to answer Lilburne's points in detail, but claimed that the special court was unquestionably legal and used 'for these many hundred years'. The judges ruled against all Lilburne's objections, Judge Keble acknowledging that he had 'spoken fair words'. He had already shown that he could perform well without a counsel.

The indictment was then read. It was of interminable length, beginning: 'Hold up thy hand, John Lilburne, thou standest here indicted of high treason...for that thou as a false traitor, not having the fear of God before thine eyes, but being stirred up and moved by the instigation of the devil, didst endeavour not only to disturb the peace and tranquility of this nation but also the government thereof to subvert.' He was accused of bringing the House of Commons 'into hatred and infamy' by writing and publishing sundry 'scandalous, poisonous and traitorous books', in which he said the government was 'tyrannical, usurped and unlawful', and of endeavouring on divers days and in divers places 'maliciously, advisedly and traitorously...to stir up a dangerous, mutinous and traitorous distemper, mutiny and rebellion in the army'.

There followed between prisoner and judges, in the words of Brailsford, 'one of the most amazing dialogues ever recorded in a court of law'. Lilburne asked for a copy of the indictment and a week's delay to study it and to subpoena witnesses, many of whom would have to travel long distances. Again and again the judges refused, only for Lilburne to come back with new arguments. In the end he gained an adjournment for one afternoon, meagre but unprecedented in a treason case, the rule being that such should end in a single day.

The next morning Lilburne did not attempt to deny that he had declared Parliament to be tyrannical or unlawful, or that he had encouraged soldiers to obtain exemption from service in Ireland. There was little doubt that, under the Treason Act, he was technically guilty. He was frankly concerned to touch the emotions of the jury and to gain their sympathy for his views. They were tradesmen, craftsmen, the stuff of which Levellers were made. They knew what unemployment was, they had suffered under the great monopolies. Lilburne told them of his service in the army, describing how he resisted the King's forces when outnumbered, and how he refused bribes when taken prisoner. He had never meditated mischief to his country, 'unless it be a mischief to oppose great men's wills'. He knew he had the support of the spectators who crowded the hall, and he exploited this. When he told the jury that it wasn't their duty to please the ciphers and clerks of the court by saying 'Amen', the people, (records the report) 'with a loud voice cried "Amen, Amen" and gave an extraordinary great hum, which made the judges look something untowardly about them', and led the general in charge 'to send for three more fresh companies of foot soldiers'. Lilburne was a bit of a showman. When the presiding judge would not allow him a short rest, he protested: 'Sir, if you will be so cruel as not to give me leave to withdraw to ease and refresh my body, I pray you, let me do it in the court. Officer, I entreat you to help me to a chamber pot.' Whereupon, we are told, 'whilst it was fetching Mr Lilburne followeth his papers and books close, and when the pot came, made water and gave it to the foreman'.

The jury retired and were back within an hour. Were they agreed on their verdict? They were. Who should speak for them? Their foreman. Then, after a command to John Lilburne to hold up his hand, 'Is he guilty of the treasons charged upon him or any of them?' 'Not guilty of all of them, nor of any one of them.' Which being pronounced (the report continues) 'the whole multitude of people in the hall, for joy of the prisoner's acquittal, gave such a loud and unanimous shout, as is believed was never heard in Guildhall, which lasted for about half an hour without intermission.' Not only in Guildhall. When Lilburne was escorted back to the Tower to await release the

> very soldiers who guarded him shouted for joy as they rode through the streets [records Brailsford], let off their pistols and in spite of their officers made the trumpeters sound *Victoria*. At the Fleet Bridge the people lit bonfires, and neither the judges nor their officers could prevail on them to put them out. As the evening wore on, the church bells rang out and bonfires sprang up all over the City, while the people in their thousands shouted and drank and feasted in the streets. The judges, one chronicler tells us, hurried home, 'like so many gadarenes . . . mocked and derided by men, women and children'.

The Levellers did not forget the jurymen to whom they owed their leader's deliverance. They presented each with a medal, on one side their name, on the other a portrait of the prisoner, with the inscription 'John Lilburne, saved by the power of the Lord and the integrity of his jury'. Overton, Walwyn and Prince were set free as well as Lilburne.

Yet, from this moment, the Leveller movement declined. The army would blow its trumpets but it would not defy its generals by electing Agitators. Without army representatives, a people's national convention would be ineffectual. Then there was a greater fear among the people than of their own oppression. The Scots were mobilizing to invade the country. Parliament, with all its faults, must be kept in being and the High Command must be supported, to repel the danger. While Lilburne had accepted a restoration of a bound monarchy, it was not to be imposed by the sword of foreigners. This was precisely what Prince Charles was preparing to do — a Scottish army in the seventeenth century was a foreign army. In addition, the prince was recruiting German and Dutch mercenaries to land in Kent and another body of invaders was to disembark at Torbay. The Levellers set aside their opposition to unite against the common enemy. They were not defeated or suppressed; they *faded* because there was no opportunity for them to function. It is difficult to convey this — an anti-climax, pathetic, a retreat into silence — after such a vociferous and heroic revival. . . There were still to be some resurrections.

Following John's narrow escape from death, his wife and brother used all their influence to induce him to abandon politics. He moved from Southwark to the City, his new neighbours nominating the hero of Guildhall to the Common Council. Cromwell became reconciled and spoke at the Council of State in favour of the payment of the compensation still due to Lilburne for his sufferings under the Star Chamber. On the initiative of Henry Marten, the Rump voted him £1,500. Lilburne could never do anything by halves. He embraced Cromwell, and, as he journeyed for his victory at Dunbar, rode with him for twenty-five miles along the Great North Road and then dined with his old adversary at Ware, no doubt in the same inn where he had awaited news of the mutiny that failed. He left with the Lord General a letter of utter loyalty. 'No man in England,' he wrote, 'shall be more forward and ready to hazard his life with you and for you, in the face of ready-to-be-discharged cannons and muskets and all the dangers of the world.' Lilburne, however, did not rejoin the army. After his brilliant performance at the Guildhall, a career at the bar beckoned him, but when he applied for admission to the Temple, his humiliated adversary, the Attorney-General, took revenge by forbidding his entrance. He did serve, however, as an amateur adviser to petitioners.

Two of these cases led Lilburne back into politics. He had no Leveller party to help him, but he could not refrain from combating injustice. In company with Major Wildman, he backed the commoners of Epworth Moor in the Fens in their claim for the restoration of 7,400 acres appropriated by the Company of Adventurers, although it had been their common land 'time out of mind'. Epworth commoners tore down a village built by the Adventurers for their Dutch workmen on the fenmen's ancestral soil. Lilburne and Wildman were each to receive a thousand acres if they succeeded in their representations – one does not recognize, comments Brailsford, the John Lilburne who used to charge only a few shillings when he pleaded a poor man's cause. He drafted for the commoners a convincing petition, but Parliament turned it down. This particular struggle between local communities (often with at least token support from their local gentry) and enclosers and profiteers from outside persisted to the next generation when Epworth parsonage was burnt down, and when the child John Wesley had to be snatched from the flames.

The second of these cases ruined Lilburne. He acted for his Uncle George in a dispute with Sir Arthur Haslerig, the Governor of Newcastle, an old enemy, in a long conflict about family estates in Durham. John signed a petition to Parliament, complaining that Haslerig had sequestered a colliery in which George was a partner. In January 1652, the Commons voted the petition false and scandalous, condemned it to be burned by the hangman, and fined George's fellow partner £7,000, committing him to prison until the fine was met. With John, the Rump dealt even more severely, seizing the opportunity to get their own back now that he was no longer a popular figure. They imposed a fine, with damages, of £7,000 and added a condemnation of death as a felon if he were found in England at the end of thirty days, shortened to twenty days by a subsequent Act of banishment. The faithful Henry Marten forced a division, but was defeated. John left for Amsterdam, and later Bruges, where he was reduced to impoverishment. Haslerig seized his land in Durham and he had to borrow for bread; his devoted wife in London had her money troubles, too. In the Low Countries, Lilburne's companions, sometimes suspicious of him as a spy, sometimes friendly, were Royalist refugees. He denied that there was an alliance between them, but he became convinced that a constitutional monarchy was best for England. Once more he broke with Cromwell.

Lilburne's mind was as active as ever. During his exile he thought out a plan which would make England great, 'honoured, courted and respected by all the neighbouring princes'. His central idea was that the two thirds of England which was common land, largely wasted, should be occupied by the landless labourers and the discharged soldiers. With stirring enthusiasm he proposed that land should be settled on every soldier and his heirs, and on 'every poor decayed housekeeper', and that provision should be made for all the old and lame past work and 'for all orphans and children that have no estate nor parents, that so in a very short time there shall not be a beggar in England, nor any idle person that hath hand or eyes, by means of all which the whole nation shall really and truly in its militia be ten times stronger, formidabler and powerfuller than now it is'. It seems to have been John's reading of Plutarch in the watches of the night which stirred his imagination, but in fact he stole the idea without acknowledgement from Dr Chamberlen's *The Poor Man's Advocate*. Lilburne sent a copy of the plan to old Levellers in Hertfordshire. At this late hour his interest in the land question and the rural proletariat was aroused. But he was isolated, exiled. What would have happened if Lilburne had been free to lead a broad-based Leveller agitation for the colonization of the wastes? Would the ex-soldiers of the New Model Army have followed him? Would the labourers in the villages have rallied to him as the craftsmen of the towns had done? We can only say it might have happened.

On 3 May 1653, Elizabeth Lilburne rejoined her husband at Bruges with the startling news that Cromwell had dissolved the Rump. They hoped this meant that John would be able to return, and Elizabeth hastened to London to seek a pass for him. It was refused. In his anger, John wrote a savage letter to Cromwell: 'It hath been your constant design to pursue my life like a partridge upon the mountains for these six or seven years together... You were the chief man who got me banished.' There was no response. After some weeks of hesitation, Lilburne decided to return to England, even if it cost him his life. He arrived in London on 14 June and petitioned Cromwell, saying he was resolved to live quietly and submissively to the government with 'my poor distressed family'. Cromwell was not appeased. The City was authorized to arrest him for felony, and two days after arrival he was imprisoned in Newgate.

Lilburne's trial at the Old Bailey was in many ways a repetition of that of the Guildhall. This time, however, the proceedings dragged on from 13 July to 20 August. By now his adversary, the Attorney-General, had become a judge and sat on the bench. Lilburne unprecedentedly was able to discuss the indictment outside court with counsel. As at the Guildhall, the case drew crowded spectators who showed 'plentiful sympathy', and, conscious of public support, he acted with startling audacity. At one point he even told the judges that he would 'cry out and appeal to the people against them'. He presented the court with an awkward dilemma. Either the Rump which banished him was a lawful Parliament or it was not. If it was a lawful Parliament, Cromwell, who broke it up by force, was the real criminal. If it was not a lawful Parliament, then the judgement it passed on him was null and void. The result of the trial was the same as at the Guildhall. The jury found him 'not guilty of any crime worthy of death'. Once more, as in 1649, 'the shouts of joy and applause were universal'. Once more the soldiers blew their trumpets and beat their drums. Lilburne was returned to Newgate to await his release.

The trial of their leader gave Leveller stalwarts an opportunity to renew activity. Cromwell tried to prejudice Parliament and the army against him by publishing reports of his intimacy with Royalists in the Low Countries. Lilburne, still confined, replied in a pamphlet which eager followers distributed, and leaflets were scattered in London streets with a new couplet:

> And what, shall then honest John Lilburne die?
> Threescore thousand will know the reason why.

Liberated, Overton and Prince rallied to him, but

Walwyn, evidently thought to be too dangerous at large, was thrown into the Tower. Prayers were offered on John's behalf in the chapels of Southwark, still a Leveller stronghold, and petitions from women, apprentices and the counties of Buckinghamshire, Hertfordshire, Bedfordshire and Kent rained on Parliament, demanding his release in accordance with the court judgment. Petitions within the army were suppressed. The agitation of protest was not so strong as in the past, but it showed that the Leveller spirit was still very much alive.

The sense of triumph on Lilburne's acquittal was short-lived. He was not released. Parliament instructed the Council of State to 'take some course' for his 'further securing', and he was transferred from Newgate to the Tower. The Council of State, deeply affronted by the verdict of not guilty, took the extraordinary step of summoning the jury before them. Most of them were craftsmen or small tradesmen – one a bookbinder, another a tallow chandler, two or three were drapers and one a brewer – from the artisan groups which gave the Levellers their strength. When questioned, they said they had returned the verdict in accordance with the dictates of conscience. The council inflicted no penalty on them, but resolved that in future political prisoners would be tried by the High Court of Justice which sat without a jury. But what would they do about John Lilburne in the Tower? They simply left him there, instructing the governor of the prison to pay no attention to any writ of *habeas corpus*. The Leveller leader could no longer use his time in prison to write pamphlets. All through the winter he was kept in 'close confinement', probably solitary confinement.

In 1651, after the Scots had been defeated at Dunbar, the forces of the King's son (after the restoration to be Charles II) were crushed by Cromwell at Worcester. The army, despite the sacking of the Agitators, was still displeased with the Long Parliament, even though the loyalists were no longer members, and called for its dissolution. This time Cromwell sided with them, and on 20 April 1653 he called in musketeers and expelled the whole House, describing them as 'corrupt and unjust men and scandalous to the profession of the Gospel'. Two months later he chose 'Godly Puritans' to take their place; his nominated Parliament was actually known as 'the Assembly of the Saints'. The Levellers protested, but now had no power against the victorious general, more powerful than any king, while their own days of any political impact were effectively over. 'The Saints' in fact proved less subservient than expected, too radical for the liking of Cromwell. A convenient *coup d'état* followed, and, subdued, a majority in the Commons surrendered all power to Cromwell, naming him Lord Protector. Nominally he was to rule with the advice of a Council of State and a Parliament, but when the Members again revolted, describing his rule as 'Egyptian bondage', he ruthlessly dismissed them and ruled as dictator. Once it was all over, he confessed his weakness and folly in having appointed 'the Saints' in the first place.

Cromwell, in a speech which surveyed his long-standing breech with the Levellers, ironically denounced them in retrospect as would-be destroyers of well-tested institutions, 'whereby England hath been known for hundreds of years'. They had wanted, he said, to undermine 'the natural magistracy of the nation' and to 'make the tenant as liberal a fortune as the landlord'. The Lord Protector, with absolute power in his hands, proceeded remorselessly to crush those with whom he had worked as colleagues. The Leveller movement, already defunct as a force, was finally dismembered, its leaders isolated in distant prisons. Under mounting pressure, the militancy of both the urban craftsmen and the rural peasants disintegrated and disappeared underground. The Levellers' revolution for democracy withered away. A glorious chapter in the struggle for freedom closed.

The fate of the heroic leaders was tragic. Overton continued his resistance even after the restoration of the monarchy with Charles II. Sent to the Tower and Chepstow Castle in 1660, he spent most of the rest of his life in prison. With only a short release, he was sentenced again in 1663 as 'suspected of seditious practices and refusing to take the oaths or give security'. Like Lilburne (still to be told) he was confined in a disciplinary prison in Jersey. The last we know of him is that he was still there in February 1668. Of the date of his death there is no trace. He was a martyr not only for democracy but also for the fact that, more than any other Leveller, he saw that social and economic freedom must accompany political freedom.

Of Walwyn's fate likewise, little is known after his release from prison in 1648, though three years later he was still publishing a pamphlet, a brave final gesture. Philosophically, he was the most modern of these three Leveller leaders, feared intellectual champion of the disfranchised, rejecting the theology of both the Episcopalians and the Puritans, a rational humanist, taking a long-term view of the futility of violence.

As for John Lilburne, Cromwell was not satisfied that the 'arch-rebel' could be silenced, even under the strict confinement imposed in the Tower. In March 1654, he was transferred to the grim fortress of Mount Orgueil Castle, built by the Normans on a rocky promontory on the island of Jersey. The Lord Protector had offered him liberty if he would engage not to act against the government, but he showed his old spirit by answering that he would 'own no way for his liberty but the way of the law'. Two months later came the last truly political statement of the Leveller leader, somehow smuggled from his prison despite severe confinement. He reflected on the evils of physical revolution. When changes took place by violence, he decided, the many who felt they were wronged do not rest 'until they find an opportunity of revenge'. He expressed a little of his life's conviction by rejecting the notion that an arbitrary government was a strong government and by saying that 'those commonwealths are weakest where injuries may be daily offered to the people by those in government'. Nevertheless, he wrote despairingly, true and perfect freedom could not be attained in this world.

Lilburne became so weak in his Channel Island dungeon that his death was reported and even described. His distraught wife, Elizabeth, was reassured by an official denial and petitioned Cromwell for his release. He was brought back to England and imprisoned at Dover Castle. Then came a development unexpected but foreshadowed by his repudiation of violence in revolution. Lilburne wrote to Elizabeth that he had become converted to Quakerism, to a firm realization that the use of force was not the means to liberty. No doubt he reached this conviction by meditation in his loneliness, perhaps accentuated by despair, but Cromwell at first declined to believe that it was sincere, interpreting the conversion as a device to escape imprisonment.

In a moving letter, Lilburne appealed to his idol of bygone days and, convinced at last, Cromwell responded — a reversal to the long love–hate relationship, which Brailsford called a son–father complex. Lilburne was unconditionally released, the Lord Protector even granting him a pension of 40s a week. The last months of the Leveller leader were described as a period of 'Quaker quietism'. He died at Eltham on 29 August 1657, and was buried at Moorfields.

Part Three:
The Diggers, 1648–51

In the seventeenth century there were, very broadly, three sections in society: the first composed of landowners and monopoly merchants, the second of small proprietors, tradesmen and skilled craftsmen, and the third of urban and rural labourers and peasants. As we have seen, the Leveller movement began within the second group, and extended only to the class of rural peasants and labourers when reflecting their grievance about the compulsory unpaid billeting of soldiers. But control remained with the urban small proprietors and their associates, whose political views reflected for the first time what was to become the traditional middle-class attitude of acclaiming political democracy while rejecting industrial democracy. They believed in the sanctity of private property and the virtue of personal acquisitiveness, and were anxious that their political action should not interfere with the economic system. Lilburne was the principal voice of this political philosophy, though in his last days he declared in favour of the massive cultivation of unoccupied common land. His colleagues, Walwyn and Overton, showed signs of inclinations towards more egalitarian and community ideas, but the dominant urban class structure of the Levellers determined their property-clinging individualist approach.

The causes for the decline of the smaller rural membership, the labourers and tenant peasants, are at present being subjected to much critical reassessment by historians. For the moment we may generalize by saying that the underpaid landless labourers were on the edge of starvation as a result of the escalating costs of the necessities of life accompanying the civil wars, while the holdings rented by the copyholders tended to be too small to yield a livelihood. They were often ruined by the tithes imposed for the upkeep of the Church, had their livestock and crops confiscated when they were too poor to pay, were imprisoned when their stocks did not yield enough, expelled from their cottages and land, which were ruthlessly grabbed by the lords of large neighbouring estates. The common people suffered; the new élite prospered.

During the period covered by this book, from the First Civil War to the Cromwell Protectorate, there was a greater seizure of land by the privileged Establishment – politicians, generals, merchants, priests, lawyers – than at any time since the confiscation of monastic properties a century earlier. According to Margaret James in *Social Policy During the Puritan Revolution*, 1,677 Royalist properties were donated to the favoured few. Speculators thrived – one dealer alone disposed of twenty-three manors. Some of the new masters took advantage of the disturbed times to expand their estates by shamelessly enclosing common land, and such gross scandals were often initiated and generally protected by the Parliament of landlords. Above all, a rapid population growth was beginning to intensify pressure on the common land available.

Three fifths of England was still common land, so designated, though much of it was used by the landlords of neighbouring estates for the grazing of cattle. While vast areas of land lay uncultivated, it has to be said that much of it was marginal in that agricultural techniques did not yet allow the possibility of its being put under the plough. The new technology would come with time, but let Brailsford describe the circumstances in which it would achieve its aims:

> Awakening...to the exciting possibilities of this problem, men reckoned that one-third of the cultivable area of England lay in such waste lands. Under their turf was buried the key to the social and economic future of England for two centuries to come. Who would find the capital and labour, animal and human, for this immense operation? Who would develop – and, it may be, appropriate – the latent riches of these acres? Not Cromwell's legions, nor Monck's, nor even Dutch William's, were as decisive a force in shaping the class structure of our island as the landlords and their lawyers who enclosed these commons. There were, as we shall see, a few far-sighted men, both Levellers and Diggers, who perceived that the operation might be organized by collective effort for the common good. In fact, the thing was done by capitalist enterprise, roughly, and with a minimum of concern for the peasants, whom it degraded to the level of a landless proletariat.

There was resistance by labourers and peasants to landlord tyranny from the beginning of the seventeenth century. In 1607 there was a rising in the Midlands against enclosures, in which, strangely, the names of 'Levellers' and 'Diggers' were first used. In the later 1620s and early 1630s revolts occurred in western England against royal enclosures of common land and the exclusion of squatters from the forests. Cromwell came into national prominence when he defended commoners who were the victims of a scheme to drain the Fens in landlord interests. But it was not until the later 1640s that the resistance gained significant proportions by the setting up of Digger colonies on common lands in a number of counties. The Diggers sought economic emancipation. They called themselves the 'True Levellers', demanding human equality in daily life. They finalized the seventeenth-century revolt. As one authority, K.V. Thomas, has written, 'the whole Digger movement can be plausibly regarded as the culmination of a century of unauthorized encroachment upon the forests and wastes by squatters and local commoners, pushed on by land shortage and pressure of population.'

The Diggers were extraordinarily fortunate in having as a champion one of the outstanding philosophers and political theorists of the seventeenth century, Gerrard Winstanley. This period was uniquely favoured by writers who sought the purpose of life and the way to live. In his *Works of Gerrard Winstanley*, G.H. Sabine says that these years saw the most extraordinary outpouring of political philosophy the modern world has known. It was, he claimed, the first of the modern revolutionary eras, 'all intellectual, religious, moral, social and political traditions broken apart and put together in a new pattern'. The list of philosophers is certainly remarkable: Thomas Hobbes, James Harrington, Henry Parker, Marchemont Nedham, Sir Robert Filmer, Anthony Ascham, George Lawson, Richard Baxter, John Locke (later), and John Milton, philosopher as well as poet. Peter Zagorin, in his *A History of Political Thought in the English Revolution*, describes Winstanley as among the greatest of them, 'one of the pre-eminent thinkers of his time'. Looking back three centuries, one can surely say that he is the most relevant to the problems of thought and politics of our present time.

There is no certainty about Winstanley's birth and up-bringing. He was probably the son of a Puritan mercer of Wigan, baptized on 10 October 1609. His later knowledge of Latin suggests that he went to a grammar school, and he became a merchant tailor. Made bankrupt during the First Civil War, he took a job pasturing cattle for Francis Drake (later his enemy) at Kingston. At first he was a Strict Baptist, but gave up attendance at church because he came to believe in 'baptism of the spirit who dwells in every creature but supremely in man'. His pantheism led him to substitute Reason for God, 'because the latter suggests a Being apart from Nature and Man', but he continued to argue from the Bible, perhaps a little opportunistically, because it was the overwhelmingly accepted last word for everyone. He states that he had a trance in which a voice commanded, 'Work together, eat bread together.' This convinced him of the truth of communism in the New Testament sense. He began to teach a revolutionary view of the Fall of Man. It occurred not when Adam and Eve were expelled from the Garden of Eden, but when Cain and Abel fought each other for property rights. Since the Universal Spirit was in all men, they must live in cooperation and equality.

The eminence of Gerrard Winstanley has been recognized in recent years. We are blessed with three detailed books about him. First there is D.W. Petergorsky's *Left Wing Democracy in the English Civil War* (Gollancz, 1940). This was followed by G.H. Sabine's monumental *The Works of Gerrard Winstanley* (Cornell University Press, 1941), completely reprinting his political tracts, accompanied by a fact-crowded introduction to the philosopher's life and thoughts. Finally, there is Christopher Hill's edition of *Gerrard Winstanley, Law of Freedom and Other Writings* (Penguin Books, 1973), which I have found the most valuable of the three, reprinting Winstanley's non-political writings (some omitted by Sabine), but also, in the introduction, relating his social analysis to the later developments of communist and socialist thinking. To each of these works, and to others less so, I am greatly indebted.

Two hundred years before Karl Marx's *Das Kapital*, Gerrard Winstanley defined the fundamental principles of socialism. His main concern was with the private ownership of land, the main economic domination, but the analysis he made applied to the vested interests of all property as opposed to community interests. He defined the conflict in society as between the acquisitive and competitive tendencies in human nature, and the tendencies for mutual aid and cooperation, and denounced any social relationship which put some in economic power over others. I cannot do better than quote Christopher Hill in his penetrating commentary. 'Winstanley postulated a primitive libertarian communism,' he writes. He cites Winstanley's dictum – 'In the beginning of time the great creator Reason made the earth to be a common treasury' and paraphrases the sequence:

> But covetousness overcame reason and equality together. A ruling class began violently to appropriate what had hitherto been common property. The earth was bought and sold. The establishment of private property led to the setting up of state power: 'the sword brought in property and holds it up, which is no other but the power of angry covetousness'. So the earth ceased to be a common treasury and became 'a place where one torments another'. Private appropriation was 'the cause of all wars, bloodshed, theft and enslaving laws that hold people under misery'. Only the abolition of private property can end 'this enmity in all hands'.

One is inclined to comment: when, before or since, was so much said in so few words?

Winstanley was outraged by 'the monopoly of land by the lords of manors. By creation-right,' he insisted, 'the land belongs to all.' He answered the objection should not 'one man be richer than another?' in passages of fine writing.

> No man can be rich [he replied] but he must be rich either by his own labours, or by the labours of other men helping him. If a man have no help from his neighbour, he shall never gather an estate of hundreds and thousands a year. If other men help him to work, then are those riches his neighbours' as well as his; for they may be the fruit of other men's labours as well as his own. But all rich men live at ease, feeding and clothing themselves by the labours of other men, not by their own; which is their shame and not their nobility; for it is a more blessed thing to give than to receive. But rich men receive all they have from the labourer's hand, and when they give they give away other men's labours, not their own. Therefore they are not righteous actors in the earth.

Winstanley had been content to theorize, but the moment came when he decided to throw in his lot with the Diggers who had begun to occupy and cultivate the common lands. No doubt he was influenced by the proposals of Peter Chamberlen, Samuel Hartlib and even Lilburne, who argued that poverty could be overcome if the often wasted unenclosed three fifths of England were fully used. Chamberlen argued that land confiscated from the Papists and Royalists should be made a 'joint stock' to benefit the poor and enrich the nation, and Lilburne popularized the idea in a grandiose plan, though he denounced the Diggers when they took direct action. Winstanley had no such doubts. In his view, the government had no democratic authority and the common land was legally the property of the people who had fought and suffered for it in the civil wars. 'England is a prison,' he wrote, 'the varieties of subtleties in the law preserved by the sword are the bolts, bars and doors of the prison; the lawyers are the jailors and poor men are the prisoners.' He was not against government, but the government of the day was not the choice of the people whom it grievously oppressed. 'If they beg they whip them by their law for vagrants,' he wrote, 'if they steal they hang them; and if they set themselves to plant the commons for a livelihood that they may neither beg nor steal, and whereby England is enriched yet will they not suffer them to do this either.'

Four days before the execution of Charles I on 30 January 1649, Winstanley decided he must act positively. He solemnly announced that 'when the Lord doth show unto me the place and manner, how he will have us that are called common people to manure and work upon the common lands, I will go forth and declare it in my action, to eat my bread with the sweat of my brows, without giving or taking hire, looking upon the land as freely mine as another.' The 'place and manner' soon became clear. On 1 April 1649, he joined the Diggers' commune on St George's Hill, at Cobham, not far from his cattle-tending at Kingston.

The Diggers' revolt is known almost exclusively by what

happened at St George's Hill, but this isolation does its extent some injustice. In several other parts of the country, labourers and peasants took over the common lands. Unfortunately, there are no detailed records such as Winstanley wrote from St George's Hill, but there is evidence of Digger activity in ten counties. The Buckingham Diggers issued their first manifesto as early as December 1648, entitling it *Light Shining in Buckinghamshire*. It called for equality in property, declaring 'all men being alike privileged by birth, so all men were to enjoy the creatures alike without property one more than the other'. In the same month, there was significantly a similar broadside from 'the Soldiers and Officers in the Regiment of Horse for the County of Northumberland', indicating that the spirit of the Agitators still lived. It is known that there were by the beginning of 1660 Digger colonies at Wellingborough in Northamptonshire, Cox Hall in Kent, Iver in Buckinghamshire, Barnet in Hertfordshire, Dunstable in Bedfordshire, Bosworth in Leicestershire, and in unnamed places in Gloucestershire and Nottinghamshire.

Despite Lilburne's criticism of them, there was considerable sympathy with the Diggers among the Levellers. Their paper, *The Moderate*, published the Buckinghamshire declaration without hostile comment, and it is interesting that a meeting of the Aylesbury Levellers in May 1649 adopted a forthright resolution of support. 'We shall help to aid and assist the poor,' they resolved, 'to the regaining of their rights, dues, etc., that do belong unto them and are detained from them by any tyrant whatsoever. And likewise will further and help the said poor to manure, dig, etc., the said Commons and to fell those woods growing thereon to help them to a stock, etc.' We may speculate that the Aylesbury Levellers knew of the Diggers at Iver near by.

The story of the Wellingborough Diggers is told so graphically in their own Declaration that we reproduce it here – as it is read, its length will be forgiven. The heading is impressive: 'A Declaration of the Grounds and Reasons why we, the Poor Inhabitants of the Town of Wellingborough in the County of

Northampton, have begun and give consent to Dig up, Manure and Sow Corn upon the Commons and Waste Ground called Bareshanke, Belonging to the inhabitants of Wellingborough, by those that have subscribed and Hundreds more that give Consent.' The first paragraph, characteristically of this Puritan period, justified action by appealing to biblical authority. 'God never gave it [the land] to any sort of people, that they should have it all to themselves and shut out all the rest, but he saith, the Earth hath been given to the children of men, which is every man.' There followed this moving statement of the reasons for the action taken:

We are necessitated from our present necessity to do this, and we hope that our Actions will justifie us in the gate, when all men shall know the truth of our necessity: We are in Wellingborough in one Parish 1169 persons to receive Alms, as the last; we have made our Case known to the Justices, the Justices have given Order that the Town should raise a Stock to set us on work, and that the Hundred should be enjoyned to assist them; but as yet we see nothing is done, nor any man that goeth about it; we have spent all we have, our trading is decayed, our wives and children cry for bread, our lives are a burden to us, divers of us having five, six, seven, eight, nine, in family, and we cannot get bread for one of them by our labor; rich men's hearts are hardened, they will not give us if we beg at their doors; if we steal, the law will end our lives, divers of the poor are starved to death already, and it were better for us that are living to die by the Sword than by the Famine: And now we consider that Earth is our Mother, and that God hath given it to the children of men, and that the common and waste Grounds belong to the poor, and that we have a right to the common ground both from the law of the Land, Reason and Scriptures; and therefore we have begun to bestow our righteous labor upon it, and we shall trust the Spirit for a blessing upon our labor, resolving not to dig up any man's propriety, until they freely give us.

There was much sympathy in Wellingborough. Contrary to their castigation of hardened hearts, the Diggers paid tribute to 'some of the rich amongst us', who, although they had profited from the common (no doubt by grazing cattle), 'have freely given us their share in it'. They also thanked 'divers country farmers' who saved seed to sow the land. The Wellingborough Diggers prospered with much local support, probably the most successful of all the common-land occupations. Research has not revealed how their brave effort was ended. No doubt they were the victims of the all-out repression to which the Cromwellian Protectorate finally resorted.

The famous St George's Hill commune, near Cobham in Surrey, was started by a pioneer Leveller, William Everard, a seasoned rebel who had been an Agitator in the army until dismissed for his radicalism. He lived at Walton-on-Thames near Winstanley, and there is evidence of visits, and of discussions between them about religion, but plans for the occupation of the common land must have been the main topic. On 1 April 1649, as we have told, the invasion began with nine intrepid volunteers, who started digging and manuring the land, designated commons but a barren heath used only for grazing the cattle of Francis Drake, Winstanley's employer, and other landowners. Three days later Winstanley joined them and the numbers grew. They erected wooden huts so that wives and children could come, becoming a community of seventy-five and later a hundred.

The dramatic story of their fortunes is told in David Caute's novel, *Comrade Jacob*: the raids by gangsters organized by the lords of the land, the burning down of their huts by troops, and the destruction of all the cultivation they had created. The Diggers' settlement was much more than an occupation of the land. It was an equalitarian commune, everyone sharing in the work, sharing good times, sharing misfortune and want. Winstanley was their inspiration, addressing them each morning in biblical terms before they began their labours, strengthening them against the Philistines who sought to destroy them. Before the end of the spring they had eleven acres of growing grain, a vegetable garden, and had built six houses.

A fortnight after Everard's occupation, information was lodged with the Council of State reciting an alarming account of the Diggers' intentions. Cromwell's chronicler, Lord Whitelocke, whom we must classify here as a hostile and hence biased witness, gave a detailed account of the alleged complaint which referred to the activity at near-by St Margaret's Hill as well as at St George's Hill:

> One Everard, once of the Army, who terms himself a Prophet, is the chief of them (one Winstanley is another chief). There were thirty men, and said that they should shortly be Four-Thousand. They invited all to come in and help them; and promised them meat, drink and clothes. They threaten to pull down park pales, and to lay all open; and threaten the neighbours that they will shortly make them all come up to the hills and work.

The President of the Council forwarded the complaint to General Fairfax with a request to send a force of horse to disperse the trespassers. At the same time the council directed the justices of the peace at Cobham to proceed against the Diggers for the 'promotion of riotous meetings'. General Fairfax sent a captain to visit the Diggers, and he reported that he found the business 'not worth the writing, nor yet taking notice of: I wonder the Council of State should be so abused of information'. The Diggers thereupon proceeded with their activities, working with dedicated enthusiasm, planning for permanent occupation, aiming to make the spring of 1650 the first achievement of an equalitarian community.

Winstanley and Everard went to see General Fairfax and, although they refused to remove their hats in his presence, 'because he was but their fellow creature', evidently won his respect, making a long declaration, read by Everard but clearly Winstanley wrote much of it. Lord Whitelocke again reported in detail. The Leveller leaders began by emphasizing the popular Puritan view that 'all the liberties of the people were lost by the coming of William the Conqueror' and that 'ever since, the people of God had lived under tyranny and oppression worse than that of our Forefathers under the Egyptians'. They continued:

> But now the time of deliverance was at hand; and God would bring His People out of this slavery, and restore them to their freedom in enjoying the fruits and benefits of the Earth. And that there had lately appeared to him, Everard, a vision; which bade him Arise and dig and plough the Earth and receive the fruits thereof. That their intent is to restore the Creation to its former condition. That as God had promised to make the barren land fruitful, so now what they did was to restore the ancient Community of enjoying the Fruits of the Earth, and distribute the benefit thereof to the poor and needy and to feed the hungry and clothe the naked. That they intend not to meddle with any man's property, nor to break down any pales or enclosures in spite of reports to the contrary; but only to meddle with what is common and untilled and to make it fruitful for the use of man. That the time will suddenly be when all men shall willingly come and give up their lands and estates and submit to the Community of Goods.

This declaration evidently impressed Fairfax. The astute appeal to Puritan patriotism against 'English bondage' under the 'Norman yoke', followed by the assurance that the Diggers had no intention of breaking into the enclosed land of neighbouring landowners, pleased the general and made him doubt whether he had cause to intervene. The most interesting feature of the declaration to those interested in the theories and plans of the Diggers is the assertion 'that the time will suddenly be' when landowners would give up their estates and join 'the Community of Goods'. Was this a definite hope of Winstanley and Everard – a three-century predecessor of the

Bhave movement in India – or a rhetorical dream? In his *Oliver Cromwell's Letters and Speeches*, written, as we have said, nearly two hundred years after these events, Thomas Carlyle took the former view. He remarked that the declaration to General Fairfax indicated that 'Everard, Winstanley and the Poor Brotherhood, who were found dibbling beans on St George's Hill under the clear April skies in 1649' were intent by their example on 'hastily bringing in a new era', not defending themselves by arms and submitting themselves to authority 'till the promised opportunity be offered, which they conceived to be at hand'.

At this point the flamboyant Everard, who had an irresistible urge to take a part in the army's struggle now reaching its climax, joined the mutinous regiments at Oxford, who were unscrupulously defeated at Burford on 14 May. This was the last we hear of him. Winstanley then became the undisputed leader at St George's Hill. He had to meet an immediate crisis. Gangsters hired by lords of the manor swarmed over the cultivated land, trampling down the seeded crops, and he had the difficult task of stimulating the depressed Diggers to begin again. Returning from Guildford to London, General Fairfax visited St George's Hill to see for himself what was happening. He was impressed by the Diggers' dedication as they planted barley to mend the devastation caused by the gangsters' raid, and was captivated by Winstanley's personality and persuasion. He became reluctant to involve the army in a dispute which, he held, was a matter for the civil authorities.

Nevertheless, early in June, soldiers joined the local landowners' mob in a heavy raid on the commune. They destroyed the crops, demolished the more permanent buildings which the Diggers had erected, and seized their spades and scythes. Under Winstanley's inspiration, the indomitable Diggers carried on. Somehow, with bare fingers, the women working by the side of the men, they cleared the ground. Winstanley wrote a strong protest to General Fairfax, describing the ill-treatment which men, women and children suffered. General Fairfax replied that the soldiers would be restrained. The promise was kept for a time. Some months later, Winstanley wrote that soldiers had not molested the Diggers.

The Diggers were seriously in need of money. With the growth of their numbers, they were ready to cultivate new land and they required funds. David Caute contrives a story, good for a novel, that Winstanley got money from the sympathetic wife of the rector of West Horsley, John Platt (about whom more later), in defiance of his orders, but so far as we know this is entertaining fiction. It is true, however, that the St George's Hill Diggers sent a mission to appeal for donations from sympathizers throughout the country, travelling to the far North, the Midlands, East Anglia and Kent, including visits to the many Digger communes. How much they raised is not known, but certainly the cultivated land expanded.

Yet the conflict between the Diggers and the landowners intensified. The Diggers began to cut down wood to rebuild their houses and to sell timber to finance the purchase of seeds and new tools. A local manifesto signed by forty-five landowners and their supporters was published, giving notice that the Diggers would be prevented from cutting more wood, and the *Mercurios Republican* reported at the end of May a 'near riot' in which horses drawing away wood were 'hurt and killed'. It was probably at this time, as told by Sabine, that a hundred Diggers were kidnapped and held in a church (that of John Platt?) until released on the order of a justice of the peace. The Diggers alleged organized hooliganism, and replied by *A Declaration of the Bloodie and Unchristian Acting* of two landowners whom they named.

More responsible landowners now decided on legal action rather than physical intervention. On 23 June, four suits asking damage for trespass were begun in the Kingston Court against the Diggers. The suits were brought by persons of standing, Lord Wenman, Sir Ralph Verney and Richard Winwood in charge of the Manor of Walton. The property affected belonged to Francis Drake, Winstanley's employer, who probably instigated the prosecution. Winstanley refused to be represented by a lawyer, instead sending to the court a statement in pamphlet form which the magistrates declined to accept. The court gave damages in the sum of £10, with costs of 29s 1d. Incongruously, the cows which Winstanley was pasturing for Drake were seized in execution of the damages, though they were subsequently returned because they were not his property. Winstanley claimed that he never paid the damages. Sabine comments that 'the purpose of the suits was not to recover damages but to harass the Diggers and break up their community'.

Their crops destroyed, their houses grounded, the Diggers decided in June to leave Francis Drake's pasturing land and to settle on unenclosed land attached to Cobham Manor, the property of the Rev. John Platt. They built four houses and planted a crop of winter grain. Trouble developed with the local traders, who, under pressure from the landlords, stopped purchasing the grain and vegetables from the Diggers. A petty riot occurred at which fifty Diggers refused to disperse at the command of the justices of the peace, and they were given notice to appear at the next quarter sessions. There was a tumultuous meeting of protest organized by the landowners in Cobham. Platt spent two weeks at army headquarters trying to persuade Fairfax to send in soldiers, but the general delayed. On 10 October, however, the Council of State directed him to do so, and he finally agreed, though he ordered moderation on the troops; they were merely to support the sheriff.

The conflict had come to a boil. In November, some soldiers joined gentry led by Platt in destroying Diggers' houses, turning out women and children onto the heath and letting loose cattle to crush the growing crops into the ground. Winstanley wrote letters of protest to General Fairfax and went to see him, but the legal process against the Diggers was nearing completion, and the general now had no option but to obey a mandatory order of the council to dispatch troops 'to close the trespassers on the hill'. The soldiers completed the destruction of the commune, crops and houses.

This time there was no hope of restoration. A court order was issued, demanding that the Diggers leave, bailiffs arrived and armed men were stationed on the devastated land. For the last time Winstanley summoned his heroic band, men and women, to a meeting among the ruined buildings, and told them that there was no alternative but to leave and to preserve their lives as best they could. They dispersed weeping.

The Public Records Office details an indictment against Winstanley and fourteen others, but it is not known with what result as no records of the Surrey Assizes are extant. They were probably indicted at the Easter quarter sessions. 'If so,' wrote Sabine, 'this was the last step in the dissolution of the communistic society at Cobham and the conclusion of Winstanley's efforts to cultivate the common land.' On 9 April 1650, Winstanley acknowledged defeat in a distressed *An Humble Request* to the Council of State.

We do not know what happened to the other Digger camps, but they, too, must have fallen under the iron hand of the lords of the manor and the state and its troops and courts. They lasted for little more than a year, perhaps not a few more than a thousand individuals were involved, but they left their mark in history as the first egalitarian endeavours in Britain. Nor is it certain what happened to Winstanley after the dissolution of the St George's Hill commune. Did the authorities press their indictment against the Diggers? If so, he may have been imprisoned. Whatever his fate, he soon proved that his equalitarian convictions persisted as strongly as ever. Realizing that the defeat of the Diggers proved that the changes he sought could not be made by groups within society, 'so long as the legal power of the landlord over the unenclosed land remained intact', he gave himself to an effort to bring about a transformation of the law.

Some eighteen months after the Cobham failure, he was moved 'to pick together' his scattered papers in a final effort to realize his aims. He addressed himself directly to Cromwell, the Lord Protector. His appeal, *The Law of Freedom*, was much more than a petition about immediate grievances. It was a comprehensive description of the New Commonwealth which he wished to see established. It outlined in detailed provisions the basis of a communist–socialist society, a successor only in British writing to More's *Utopia*. It is a work of historic importance still little recognized.

Winstanley agreed in his introduction that there were two ways of ordering the earth: either by private ownership and 'the cheating art of buying and selling', or by communal ownership without buying and selling. He wrote that existing governments depended on private ownership, on war and conquest, and on the domination of some men over others by force and fraud. His pattern for a communist social organization may seem naïve to us, but it was written nearly two centuries before the Industrial Revolution and within economic conditions which were relatively primitive, mostly involving the land and its products. He did not forget the manufacturing elements then evolving. He advocated a state monopoly of foreign trade and the collective use of labour, industry and inventions. His concentration on the land problem was partly a result of his own experience, but it also reflected the fact that land was then the dominant feature of private ownership.

His basic plan of economic organization was that crops when harvested, and all goods when manufactured, should be placed in public storehouses, some wholesale and some retail, from which they would be distributed without charge to all who needed them either for their own consumption or as raw material for future processing. The system would be regulated by making it criminal to be idle, wasteful or inactive in a useful trade. There would be overseers to guide the best processes for producing goods, what goods were needed, and what quantities were required. Their functions would also include the encouragement of research and arts and crafts. Everyone should be taught a trade which would be of value to the community.

The picture of a new society was not limited to economic relations. At a time when the clergy, to use Christopher Hill's phrase, were 'society's ideologists and educators', propagandists for the establishment, he boldly declared for the separation of the Church and state, leaving each congregation free to elect its own minister. Education would be taken out of clerical hands and made scientific, equal and universal. Winstanley rejected all élitism and privilege, and insisted that science should be directed to improving not only economic conditions but the quality of life. He was a socialist before socialism. His plea to Cromwell had little effect, but the principles he taught have now become the faith of millions in the world.

To the Diggers, their communism was not merely a way of better material conditions. It was a way of life. They expressed their belief in equality by their spirit of service and cooperation. They were not solemn do-gooders. They must have enjoyed laughter and fun, as expressed in the songs of Robert Coster. Here are some verses from their favourite song, which the poet named after them:

The Diggers' Song

You noble Diggers all, stand up now, stand up now,
 You noble Diggers all, stand up now,
The waste land to maintain, seeing Cavaliers by name
Your digging does disdain, and persons all defame.
 STAND UP NOW, STAND UP NOW.

Your houses they pull down, stand up now, stand up now,
 Your houses they pull down, stand up now.
Your houses they pull down to fright poor men in town,
But the gentry must come down, and the poor shall wear
 the crown.
 STAND UP NOW, DIGGERS ALL.

With spades and hoes and ploughs, stand up now, stand
 up now,
 With spades and hoes and ploughs, stand up now,
Your freedom to uphold, seeing cavaliers are bold
To kill you if they could, and rights from you to hold.
 STAND UP NOW, DIGGERS ALL.

The gentry are all round, stand up now, stand up now,
The gentry are all round, stand up now.
The gentry are all round, on each side they are found,
This wisdom's so profound, to cheat us of our ground.
STAND UP NOW, STAND UP NOW.

The lawyers they conjoin, stand up now, stand up now,
The lawyers they conjoin, stand up now.
To arrest you they advise, such fury they devise,
The devil in them lies and hath blinded both their eyes.
STAND UP NOW, STAND UP NOW.

The clergy they come in, stand up now, stand up now,
The clergy they come in, stand up now.
The clergy they come in, and say it is a sin
That we should now begin, our freedom for to win.
STAND UP NOW, DIGGERS ALL.

To conquer them by love, come in now, come in now,
To conquer them by love, come in now.
To conquer them by love, as it does you behove,
For he is King above, no power is like to love.
GLORY HERE, DIGGERS ALL.

They sang these words in rhythm as they dug and sowed
and reaped.

THE
TRYAL
Of Lieutenant Colonel
John Lilburn.

By an Extraordinary or Special Commiſſion, of *Oyer*
and *Terminer* at the *Guild-Hall* of *London*, the 24th,
25th, and 26th. of *October*, 1649.

Being exactly Pen'd and taken in Short-Hand, as it
was poſſible to be done in ſuch a Croud and Noiſe,
and Tranſcribed with an Indifferent and Even Hand,
both in Reference to the Court, and the Priſoner;
that ſo Matter of Fact, as it was there Declared,
might truly come to Publick View.

In which is contain'd the Names of all the Judges, Grand
Inqueſt, and Jury of Life and Death.

By THEODORUS VARAX,

𝕿𝖍𝖊 𝕾𝖊𝖈𝖔𝖓𝖉 𝕰𝖉𝖎𝖙𝖎𝖔𝖓.

Eſther 4. verſ. 13. and Iſ. 12. verſ. 2, 3, 4.

*Then Mordecai commanded to anſwer Eſther, Think not with thy ſelf that
thou ſhalt eſcape in the King's Houſe, more then all the Jews. Behold,
God is my Salvation: I will truſt and not be afraid, for the LORD
JEHOVAH is my Strength, and my Song, he alſo is become my Salvation. Therefore with joy ſhall ye draw water out of the wells of Salvation. And in that Day ſhall you ſay, Praiſe the LORD, call upon
his Name, declare his doings among the People, make mention that his
Name is exalted.*

Enter'd in the Hall-Book of the Company of *Stationers*, purſuant to Act
of Parliament.

London : Printed for and Sold by *H. Hills*, in *Black-fryars*.

A
DISCOVRSE

Betwixt

LIEUTENANT COLONEL

IOHN LILBURN

Clofe Prifoner in the Tower of *London,*

AND

Mr HUGH PETER:

Upon *May* 25. 1649.

Publifhed by a friend, for the Publick benefit.

MAT. 7. 15, 16.
*Beware of falfe Prophets, which come to you in Sheeps clothing, but inwardly they are ravening Wolves.
Ye shall know them by their fruits: Do men gather grapes of thorns, or figs of thiftles ?*

LONDON,
Printed in the Yeer 1649.

THE
Declaration and Standard

Of the *Levellers* of *England*;
Delivered in a Speech to his Excellency the Lord Gen. *Fairfax*,
on *Friday* laſt at White-Hall, by Mr. *Everard*, a late Member of the
Army, and his Propheſie in reference thereunto; ſhewing what will
befall the Nobility and Gentry of this Nation, by their ſubmitting to
community; With their invitation and promiſe unto the people, and
their proceedings in *Windſor* park, *Oatlands* park, and ſeverall other
places; alſo, the Examination and confeſſion of the ſaid Mr. *Everard*
before his Excellency, the manner of his deportment with his Hat on,
and his ſeverall ſpeeches and expreſſions, when he was commanded
to put it off. Together with a Liſt of the ſeverall Regiments of Horſe
and Foot that have caſt Lots to go for *Ireland*.

Imprinted at *London*, for *G. Laurenſon*, *Aprill* 23. 1649.

A Manifestation

FROM

Lieutenant Col. *John Lilburn*, Mr. *William Walwyn*, Mr. *Thomas Prince*, and Mr. *Richard Overton*,

(Now Prisoners in the Tovver of *London*)
And others, commonly (though unjustly)

STYLED

LEVELLERS.

Intended for their

FVLL VINDICATION

FROM

The many aspersions cast upon them, to render them odious to the World, and unferviceable to the *Common-wealth*.

And to fatisfie and afcertain all MEN whereunto all their Motions and Endeavours tend, and what is the ultimate Scope of their Engagement in the

PVBLICK AFFAIRES.

They also that render evill for good, are *Our* adverfaries: becaufe we follow the thing that good is.

Printed in the year of our LORD, 1649.

The Army's Martyr:

OR

A more ful RELATION of the barbarous and illegall Proceedings of the Court-Martiall at *WHITE-HALL*

UPON

Mr. ROBERT LOCKIER:

Who was shot to death in Paul's *Church-yard,*
upon the 27 *day of* April, 1 6 4 9.

And a brief Narrative of the Cause thereof.

VVith his Christian carriage and deportment, and
his dying SPEECHES to all his fellow-souldiers at the
time of his Execution, as an everlasting
witnesse of his integrity to the Rights
and Freedoms of the
COMMON--WEALTH.

WITH

A PETITION

Of divers well-affected persons,

AND A LETTER

Of Lieut. Col. *Jo. Lilburn,* and M. *Ri. Overton,*
Presented
To the GENERAL in his behalf.

1 KING. 2. 5, 6.
The blood of War shed in the time of Peace,
Cries out for vengeance ; or our Freedoms cease.

Printed at *London* in the Yeer 1 6 4 9.

The Triumph stain'd.

Being an ANSWER to
TRUTHS TRIUMPH,
i.e. a Pamphlet so called, and lately set forth
By Mr. *John Wildman,*
a pretended Gentleman of the Life-guard to his
Excellency Sir *Tho: Fairfax.*

WITH

A full and perfect Account of an

INFORMATION

OF

Dangerous and bloody consequence, given in
to the House of Lords (at their Bar) January
the 18. 1647. against Lieut. Col. *Iohn
Lilburn* and John *Wildman.*

By *George Masterson*, Preacher of the
Gospel at *Shoreditch* near *London.*

1 COR. 4. 5.
*Therefore judge nothing before the time, until the Lord come, who both
will bring to light the hidden things of darkness, and will make ma-
nifest the counsels of the hearts: and then shall every man have
praise of God.*

London, Printed by JOHN FIELD. 1647.

A DECLARATION

TO THE

Powers of England,

AND

To all the Powers of the VVorld, shewing the Cause why the common People of England have begun, and gives consent to dig up, manure, and sow Corn upon *George-Hill* in *Surrey* ; by those that have subscribed, and thousands more that give consent.

OR,

The state of Community opened, and presented to the Sons of Men.

BY

William Everard,	*Christopher Clifford,*	*William Hoggrill,*
Iohn Palmer,	*Iohn Barker,*	*Robert Sawyer,*
Iohn South,	*Ferrard Winstanley,*	*Thomas Eder,*
Iohn Courton,	*Richard Goodgroom,*	*Henry Bickerstaffe,*
William Taylor,	*Thomas Starre,*	*Iohn Taylor, &c.*

Beginning to plant, and manure the wast Land upon *George-Hill,* neare *Walton,* in the County of *Surrey.*

LONDON,

Printed for *Giles Calvert,* at the Black Spread-Eagle at the West end of *Pauls.* 1649.

AN
APPEAL
To the House of
COMMONS,

Desiring their ANSVVER:

VVhether the Common - people
shall have the quiet enjoyment of the
Commons and *Waste Land*;

Or whether they shall be under the will of
Lords of *Mannors* still.

Occasioned by an Arrest, made by *Thomas* Lord
Wenman, *Ralph Verny* Knight, and *Richard Winwood* Esq;
upon the Author hereof, for a Trespass, in Digging
upon the Common-Land at *Georges* Hill in *Surrey*.

By *Gerrard Winstanly*, *Iohn Barker*, and *Thomas*
Star, In the Name of all the poor oppressed
in the Land of E N G L A N D.

Unrighteous Oppression kindles a flame; but Love, Righteous-
ness, and Tenderness of heart, quenches it again.

Printed in the Year, 1649.

Conclusions

Are we justified in calling the Levellers, Agitators and Diggers the first British socialists? They all certainly contributed to the concept of *democratic* socialism. The Levellers were pioneers of political democracy and the sovereignty of the people; the Agitators were the pioneers of participatory control by the ranks at their workplace; and the Diggers were pioneers of communal ownership, cooperation and egalitarianism. The three together equate with democratic socialism.

The opponents of socialism often identify it with state authoritarianism. That is emphatically not true. Karl Marx looked forward to the withering away of the state, though he justified the dictatorship of the proletariat during the transition from capitalism to communism. Unhappily, 'communist' states have used a prolonged transition to suppress freedom of expression, but democratic socialists passionately believe that liberty of thought is the necessary condition for progress and the realization of truth. It is significant that the communist parties of Western Europe now accept democratic liberties, and the experiences of Portugal and Spain suggest that draconian suppression is not necessary even during transition from fascism. Democratic socialism is in the ascendancy.

When one thinks about it, democracy emerges as the essence of socialism. Democracy has been regarded as the best available means of government. That is not enough. Government, though it affects us all, is distant. In a truly democratic society, the people would control their lives in all daily experience. Workers when they enter a factory today do not feel it is *theirs*. It is owned by others or, if nationalized, is managed by others. They exert pressure through their trade unions, but this is confrontation, 'we' and 'they'. Democracy requires not only common ownership, but conscious participation in administration by all engaged, trade unions becoming constructive partners. This is industrial democracy supplementing political democracy.

So many of the conflicts which plague our life are due to the absence of participating democracy. Strikes. Establish industrial democracy, with workers actually partners in decisions, part of the management from shop floor to the top board, and industrial disputes would become rare. Cooperation in practice is the answer to confrontations. Controversy should continue. It is the condition of progress. But not without democratic participation.

Democratic socialism would expand participation not only to workers in industry but to every sphere of life; consumers' associations with a voice in the running of public services and the price of goods, local social activities participating in sharing in the administration of the local authority including the many voluntary organizations where members already function cooperatively. Why should not tenants' associations participate in the administration of their estates?

Socialism, above everything else, is democracy in life, cooperation by all in every activity which requires working together, becoming conscious participation by everyone in a harmonized society to which all feel they belong. That demands the creation of the spirit of socialism as well as its body. Socialism *is* democracy. This is why the Levellers are so important. It is noteworthy that they began with an assertion of the principle of toleration for all religious beliefs. Toleration is the ethical basis of democracy.

The Levellers were the earliest grouping in this country – incredibly, three centuries ago – to realize the importance of democracy. In his *The Levellers in the English Revolution*, Professor Aylmer writes that the Levellers were 'the first democratic political movement in modern history. Indeed, it is fair to say that until the later eighteenth century in America, Britain and France they were unique.' They enshrined democracy as their overriding principle not only for Parliament, including the abolition of the House of Lords and the monarchy (until Cromwell became a greater menace to democracy than a king), but for the Church, the judiciary, local government, public offices, even the army. They were aware of the danger that an elected Parliament might usurp excessive powers, insisting that sovereignty lay with the people and calling for a Charter of Rights which would bind even the legislature. Their one doubt was in their definition of electoral democracy as manhood suffrage. Did they mean to include women? Was the phrase used as we use 'one man, one vote' when we mean adult suffrage including women?

The Levellers not only advocated democracy for society, they applied it to their own organization, again extraordinarily in the far-away seventeenth century when authoritarianism and bureaucracy were the order of the day. They established for the first time something approximating to what we understand as being a political party, with all the inner democracy which modern parties boast (not with absolute credence). They had their ward groups meeting in the social units of the people, the taverns (some of which still exist as old-time public houses – I would have plaques placed on their walls in commemoration). The ward parties appointed representatives to a central council, which in turn appointed an executive. Each member was required to subscribe to local and national funds. The one evident qualification of this inner democracy was that too much power continued to remain with the urban members when the Levellers extended their membership to peasants and rural labourers and to the miners in the Midlands.

This party democracy worked. Activity was a model which parties today rarely attain. During all their prolonged struggle, ward groups and council and executive were in almost daily session, meeting after working hours, no doubt to the early hours of next morning. Only during the 1926 General Strike did we achieve that in modern times! An astonishing feature was the speed with which each section of the party worked – petitions printed at an underground press, 10,000 signatures collected in two days, presented to Parliament the third day; pamphlets by their leaders continuously smuggled from prison, printed clandestinely, distributed widely not only among civilians but through contacts in the regiments of the army scattered all over the country; the massive turn-out at marches organized on an immediate issue within a few hours. This reflected, of course, the urgent enthusiasm which arose from continuous crises – the fact that makes their story so exciting – but it is surprising how long the dedication lasted. The Levellers gave the example for every revolution which has followed.

The Levellers were more than revolutionary. They were constructive in depth. They were the first to call for a whole series of reforms, civil, social and economic, some now an accepted part of our life, some expanded, some still to be realized, a few admittedly irrelevant and even unacceptable. The list of the main objectives they took the initiative in urging is breath-taking:

Tolerance towards all religions and to none, freedom to worship according to convictions, abolition of tithes to maintain the State Church.

Democratization of the Legislature by 'manhood' suffrage, fixed periods of Parliament, the abolition of the House of Lords, the abolition of the monarchy (later, a constitutional monarchy rather than a dictator).

Decentralization of the administration, control of social services by elected local authorities, election of judges and public officers.

Decentralization of the army, appointment of representatives to a central council by each regiment, nomination of commanding officers by the government. Allocation to local authorities of forces to be raised, election of local officers, no conscription for service overseas (advocated in association with the Agitators).

No enclosure by landlords of common land, transformation of tenancies requiring obligations to landlords into freeholds, mass cultivation of common lands (Lilburne in final stage).

Control of monopolies in foreign trade.

Free education (only for boys?), provision of hospitals, and accommodation for the distressed, the sick, the disabled, widows, orphans and aged at public expense under local control.

The right to work and a living wage (arising from miners' strike).

A Charter of Rights ('Agreement of the People') which would have authority over Parliament.

Opposition to imperialism, exampled particularly in resistance to the reoccupation of Ireland.

To some of the above proposals incidentals were added which would be unacceptable today, perhaps even ridiculous, but which were appropriate at the time. For example, the Levellers asked that the entire electorate of a parish should select the clergy of the State Church – absurd now, but not so inappropriate when attendance at church was compulsory and when the clergy were the main source of news and views. The Levellers declared against the re-election of a Member of Parliament: one term was enough. How many statesmen of renown would have been eliminated had this rule been observed! But the common people of the seventeenth century had experience of corrupt politicians clinging to power for long periods, and the Levellers thought of Parliament not so much as a place for initiating decisions as for recording the decisions of those who elected it. Let leaders put their views to the people, but it was the views of the people, not of the leaders, which should count. They were committed democrats, even to the point of believing in delegation rather than representation.

Putting these and other incidentals aside, it is difficult to think of any movement in any period of history which has set so many precedents as the Levellers did. They were a political phenomenon, largely failing in their own time, but pioneers of many tomorrows. Above all, they were pioneers of the principle of democracy which, we have argued, is the core of socialism.

The Agitators took the process a stage further. How far they were the agents of the Levellers in the army, how far they were spontaneous and by contact influenced the Levellers outside, we do not know. Probably it was a bit of each, but, whichever it was, their place in social history is immensely important. They were the first to apply democracy to the place of their employment. It is not really significant that this happened to be the unusual scene of the army. The New Model Army inherited from the civil wars against King Charles was not an institution distinct and distant from the people. It *was* the people, the activists among them, many volunteers, eagerly involved in everything that happened. It was natural, therefore, that they should express their views, assert themselves, ask that they be consulted when decisions affecting not only their lives but the life of the nation were concerned.

In addition, they were a power in the land, not merely because they had arms but because they were a large-scale employment force, equivalent to the thousands of workers in a large company today, then unique because industry and services were small-based. They were potentially the strongest pressure group in the country. It was their military power which intimidated Parliament and the City of London, but it was the view of the massed ranks which decided how that power was used. All through history, armies have dominated society, overthrowing governments, imposing dictatorships. But this was something different. It was a demand within the army not for power for itself but for power for the whole people, for democracy.

Let us turn from this momentous fact to the actual instrument used. Each regiment elected two representatives to serve side by side with the commanding officers on the Army Council, and this council decided all action. In Putney Church, which should be consecrated as a cathedral of democracy, a parliament of the whole army met and freely debated its course of action, the corporal having as much opportunity as the commander. A unique event. The Agitators did not then see the precedent they were setting. They were the first shop stewards, representing the men on the barrack floor, the ancestors of the shop stewards representing the men on the factory floor today.

This was the significant gift of the Agitators to social history. They represented the claim of the ranks to participate in the decisions of the organization in which they were employed. It happened to be the army (the last institution where the principle is likely to be accepted in these times), but the principle applies wherever men and women are employed. Partnership in control of their own work-life and in the purposes to which it is devoted — that is the revolutionary precedent the Agitators set. Work-place democracy, forerunner of industrial democracy.

So to the Diggers. They were the third stage, the completion to the realization of personal freedom, common ownership, equality, cooperation and human fulfilment, the fundamentals of democratic socialism. A full description has already been given of the philosophy of their inspired interpreter Gerrard Winstanley; he should be canonized as a saint of socialism. He was not the first in Britain to describe the pattern of a communist society. That honour belongs to Thomas More, who, at the time of writing these conclusions (on the occasion of the 500th anniversary of his book) is being commemorated as a saint of Catholicism. Christopher Hill in his work on Winstanley points to the difference between him and More. *Utopia* was written in Latin, the language of the intellectual élite, a fantasy, perhaps a *jeu d'esprit*, not a manifesto to imitate, not a Bible for behaviour and action. Dr Hill may be a little unfair to More in suggesting that, as Lord Chancellor, he was inconsistent in having 'a short way with the radical revolutionaries of his own day'. The charge was made that, among other penalties, he flogged 'heretics' in his custody. From his cell in the Tower of London just before his execution, More insisted that he had ordered flogging on only one man, for the offence of putting his hands up women's skirts in church during the elevation of the host.

Socialists today should join the tributes to Thomas More, but there is truth in the distinction drawn between him and Gerrard Winstanley. In all his pamphlets the Diggers' advocate called on the oppressed poor to action, to seize and cultivate the common lands and to establish egalitarian societies on them. His *Law of Freedom*, outlining the communist order of his dreams, was a serious appeal to Cromwell to supplement the overthrow of kingly power by building the basis of a just New Commonwealth. He wrote before the Industrial Revolution, and there is force in Christopher Hill's suggestion that his proposals should be studied in the Third World, similar, today, in many respects to seventeenth-century Britain. Indeed, Julius Nyerere's village socialism in Tanzania is close to the communities constructed by the Diggers on the wasted unenclosed heaths. Winstanley was the father of British socialism, action wedded to theory, 200 years before Robert Owen, William Morris or Karl Marx. We have failed to acknowledge him as such.

The Diggers not only held socialist principles, but they put them into practice. Let us try to capture in imagination the conditions when Cromwell assumed the Protectorate. Political chaos: the King executed, the reactionary self-perpetuating majority in Parliament dismissed, military rule by the army commanders, the Agitators crushed. Economic crisis: the devastation caused by the two civil wars and by the war against the Irish, a peasantry driven from their little holdings and cottages because they could not pay their tithes, their land enclosed by the lords of the manor, starving land-less labourers, their families without the bread for which they should be growing the grain.

It was in this situation that Chamberlen and Lilburne urged that the wasted common lands should be handed over to the hungry peasants and labourers to be cultivated. Simul-taneously, the True Levellers, grouped in many parts of the country, in the North, the Midlands, East Anglia, the Home Counties and the South, came to the same conclusion, and they acted on it.

Their assertions amounted, at least in embryo, to an attempt at a socialist revolution. Wherever the common lands were occupied, egalitarian communities were established, all working, all sharing. Bravely they withstood the raids of gangsters recruited by the landlords angry that the common land which they had arrogated for the grazing of their cattle should be used in common; bravely they began again when their crops were destroyed and their simple accommodation razed to the ground by troops. Finally, by the intervention of the state and the courts, they were defeated. But what a heroic story!

Winstanley came to see that direct action by groups must fail against the powers of the state. He supplemented Thomas More's *Utopia* by submitting the details of a *New Common-wealth* to Cromwell for his consideration. His socialist plan may seem naïve today, with all the complexities which have followed the Industrial Revolution and the world financial system; but the principles of socialism were there, asserted for the first time in the name of the thousand and more who had acted and suffered for their faith. Socialists of today, still more the socialists of tomorrow when they achieve, should cherish and keep alive the memory of the Diggers as their fore-fathers, their ancestors.

We end as we began by asking whether we are right to

acclaim the Levellers, the Agitators and the Diggers as the first British socialists.

The Levellers were the pioneers of political democracy.
The Agitators were the pioneers of work-place democracy.
The Diggers were the pioneers of economic democracy.

That surely adds up to democratic socialism.

We have quoted from Thomas Carlyle. In his book on Cromwell he gave a final judgement on the Levellers and Diggers.

Levelling, in the practical civil and military provinces of English things, is forbidden to be. In the spiritual provinces it cannot be forbidden; for there it everywhere already is. It ceases dibbling beans on St George's Hill near Cobham; ceases galloping in mutiny across the Isis to Burford — takes into Quakerism, and Kingdoms which are not of this world.

This is a tribute to eternal values, but a century beyond Carlyle as we look back on the Levellers and the True Levellers is it not for us to determine, with the hope of what has already been achieved, that it is in this world that their principles of democracy and equality shall be realized? They were the first British socialists. How long will it be before a Brailsford or Christopher Hill writes *Britain's Triumphant Socialism?*

Selected Reading List

Background

R. Ashton, *The English Civil War: Conservatism and Revolution 1603–1649*, Weidenfeld & Nicolson, 1978. The most recent political history of the period.

B. Manning, *The English People and the English Revolution*, Heinemann, 1976; Peregrine 1978. Concentrates on the radical revolution; provides a valuable discussion of the Levellers within this tradition.

C. Hill, *The World Turned Upside Down*, Temple Smith, 1972; Pelican, 1975. Exciting study which discusses Levellers and Diggers and other radical groups against the background of the radical revolution.

The Levellers

H.N. Brailsford, *The Levellers and the English Revolution*, ed. C. Hill, Cresset Press, 1961; Spokesman Books, 1976. A magisterial study.

J. Frank, *The Levellers*, Harvard UP, 1955. A study of the

movement written essentially around the writings of its leading spokesmen.

H. Shaw, *The Levellers*, Longmans, 1968. A short, recent study.

There are biographies of several of the Leveller leaders:

P. Gregg, *Free-born John. A Biography of John Lilburne*, Harrap, 1961. Well-informed and highly readable.

M. Ashley, *John Wildman*, Cape, 1947.

H. Ross Williamson, *Four Stuart Portraits*, Evans Brothers, 1949. Includes a biography of Colonel Thomas Rainsborough.

The Diggers

L. Behrens, *The Digger Movement in the Days of the Commonwealth*, 1906, reprinted Holland & Merlin Press, 1961

D. Petegorsky, *Left-Wing Democracy in the English Civil War*, Gollancz, 1940. Old but valuable short study published by the Left Book Club.

Other Radical Groups

B. Capp, *Fifth Monarchy Men*, Faber, 1972

P.G. Rogers, *The Fifth Monarchy Men*, Oxford Universty Press, 1966

A.L. Morton, *The World of the Ranters*, Lawrence & Wishart, 1970; paperback, 1979. Includes chapter on the Levellers.

Documents

Readers who wish to sample the vigorous prose of the radical pamphleteers are well-served.

Leveller Manifestoes of the Puritan Revolution, ed. Don M. Wolfe, Nelson, 1944; reprinted 1967

The Leveller Tracts, 1647–1653, ed. W. Haller & G. Davies, Columbia University Press, 1944; reprinted 1964

The Works of Gerrard Winstanley, ed. G.H. Sabine, Cornell University Press, 1941. Useful introduction and prints valuable collection of documents relating to the Diggers.

These are the standard collections. More accessible collections of documents are to be found in the following:

A.S.P. Woodhouse, ed., *Puritanism and Liberty*, Dent, Second edition 1950

G.E. Aylmer, ed., *The Levellers in the English Revolution*, Thames & Hudson, 1975

A.L. Morton, ed., *Freedom in Arms. A Selection of Leveller Writings*, Lawrence & Wishart, 1978

C. Hill, ed., *Winstanley: The Law of Freedom and other Writings*, Pelican, 1973. Valuable introduction.

Articles

The radical groups of the 1640s continue to fascinate historians and research on them actively continues. Here are some of the most recent contributions:

C.B. Macpherson, *The Political Theory of Possessive Individualism*, Oxford University Press, 1962; paperback 1964. Macpherson's radical questioning of how extensive Leveller proposals were for the franchise has stimulated a lively debate.

C. Webster, ed., *The Intellectual Revolution of the Seventeenth Century*, Routledge & Kegan Paul, 1974. Conveniently reprints most of the more recent articles on the radical groups.

K. Thomas, 'The Levellers and the Franchise' in G.E. Aylmer, ed., *The Interregnum: the Quest for Settlement 1646–1660*, Macmillan, 1972. The most important recent contribution to the debate.

Author's Bibliography

BOOKS

Labour and Liberalism, The National Labour Press, 1910

Socialism for Pacifism, N.L.P., 1917

India and its Government, (Labour Booklet No. 6) The Labour Publishing Co., 1921

English Prisons To-day, (with Stephen Hobhouse), Longman's, Green and Co., 1922

A New Way With Crime, Williams and Norgate Ltd, 1928

The Indian Crisis, Victor Gollancz Ltd, 1930

Hungry England, Victor Gollancz Ltd, 1932

The Bloody Traffic, Victor Gollancz Ltd, 1933

Will Roosevelt Succeed?, George Routledge and Sons, 1934

Purple Plague: A Tale of Love and Revolution, Sampson Low and Marston and Co. Ltd, 1935

Workers Front, Martin Secker and Warburg Ltd, 1934

Inside the Left: Thirty Years of Platform, Press, Prison and Parliament, A Political Autobiography, George Allen and Unwin Ltd, 1942

Death Pays a Dividend, (with Frederic Mullally), Victor Gollancz Ltd, 1944

German Diary, Victor Gollancz Ltd, 1946

Socialism Over Sixty Years: The Life of Jowett of Bradford,
George Allen and Unwin Ltd, 1946

Bermondsey Story: The Life of Alfred Salter, George Allen
and Unwin Ltd, 1949

African Journeys, Victor Gollancz Ltd, 1955

Red Liner: A Novel in T.V. Form, (an adaptation of *Purple
Plague*), Lawrence and Wishart, 1961

Outside the Right, George Allen and Unwin Ltd, 1963

African Socialism: A Background Book, The Bodley Head,
1964

Immigration: What is the Answer?, Two Opposing Views,
(with Norman Pannell), Routledge and Kegan Paul, 1965

Women Against the Desert, (with Miss W. Campbell-Purdie),
Victor Gollancz Ltd, 1967

The Shrinking Explosive World, The Epworth Press, 1967

The Colonial Revolution, Hart-Davis MacGibbon Ltd, 1973

Towards Tomorrow (autobiography), Hart-Davis
MacGibbon Ltd, 1977

PAMPHLETS

'What the I.L.P. Wants.' The National Labour Press Ltd, 1914

'Is Britain Blameless?' (Speech 21 Jan. 1915) The National
Labour Press Ltd, 1915

'The Devil's Business. A play and its justification.' The National Labour Press Ltd, 1915

'Why I am a Conscientious Objector.' (Being Answers to the
Tribunal Catechism) (With Others.) The No-Conscription
Fellowship, 1916

'The Recruit. A Play in One Act.' The National Labour Press
Ltd, 1918

'Prisons as Crime Factories.' I.L.P. New Series No.21, 1919

'Can Britain Disarm?' No More War Movement, 1920

'All About the I.L.P.' I.L.P., 1920

'Non-Cooperation in Other Lands.' Tagore and Co.,
Madras, 1921

'Lloyd George and the Traffic in Honours.' I.L.P., 1922

'How to End War.' (The I.L.P. View on Imperialism and Internationalism) I.L.P., 1925

'Make the Workers Free!' (The Industrial Policy of the I.L.P.) I.L.P., 1925

'The Devil's Business.' (New Edition) I.L.P., 1926

'A Week in India (And Three Months in an Indian Hospital)' The New Leader Ltd, 1928

'Socialism – With Speed!' (An Outline of the I.L.P. 'Socialism in Our Time' Proposals) I.L.P., 1928

'India's Challenge.' I.L.P., 1930

'The I.L.P. and the Crisis.' I.L.P., 1931

'The Anomalies Bill. Why its Rejection was moved.' (Speeches in Parliament) (With Others) I.L.P., 1931

'A Socialist Plan for Unemployment.' (Speech. 16 April 1931) I.L.P., 1931

'Hands off the Railmen's Wages!' (A Scathing Exposure of the Capitalist Control of the Railways, with a startling Who's Who of the Railway Directors) I.L.P., 1931

'The Coming Revolution.' I.L.P., 1932

'Which Way for the Workers?' (Debate with Harry Pollitt. 18 April 1932) C.P. of G.B., 1932

'Socialism at the Cross Roads.' (Why the I.L.P. left the Labour Party) I.L.P., 1932

'The Next Step Towards Working-class Unity.' (Speech at I.L.P. Conference, Derby, 1933) I.L.P., 1933

'Profits from Blood. The War-Makers Exposed.' I.L.P., 1935

'Italy and Abyssinia. Should British Workers Take Sides?' (With Others) I.L.P., 1936

'The Truth About Barcelona.' I.L.P., 1937

'Pacifism and the Left Wing.' Pacifist Publicity Unit, 1938

'End the War by a Real Peace.' (With C.A. Smith) I.L.P., 1939

'Socialism Can Defeat Nazism.' (With John McNair) I.L.P., 1940

'The Way Out.' I.L.P., 1942

'Stop the War by Socialism.' I.L.P., 1942

'Cat and Mouse. The Repeated Prosecution of Conscientious Objectors.' Central Board of Conscientious Objectors, 1942

'Break Truce with Tories and Build Labour Unity!' (A Statement for consideration by men and women of the Labour Movement) (With James Maxton) I.L.P., 1943

'The C.O. and the Community.' (Speech) Fellowship of Conscientious Objectors, 1943

'5 points for the British People.' (With Others) I.L.P., 1946

'Empire in Crisis. A survey of conditions in the British Colonies Today.' A Peace News Pamphlet, 1953

'Why Mau Mau?' The Movement for Colonial Freedom, 1953

'Waging Peace. The need for a change in British Policy.' (With Richard Acland & Leslie Hale) Peace News Series, 1954

'1960. Africa's Year of Destiny. A Political Guide to a Continent in Crisis.' Movement for Colonial Freedom, 1960

'Let Britain Lead. The Case for Labour's New Defence Policy.' (With Others) Campaign for Nuclear Disarmament, 1960

'What is the M.C.F.?' The Movement for Colonial Freedom.

'The White Dictators of Southern Rhodesia.' The Movement for Colonial Freedom, 1962

'Fennér Brockway's Eightieth Birthday Celebrations.' (Speech). The Movement for Colonial Freedom, 1968

'Next Step to Peace.' London Coop Political Committee, 1970

'Peace Within Reach.' (With Others) Committee for European Security and Cooperation, 1973

'A Great Hope for Peace.' London Coop Political Committee, 1974

'The Hope for Peace.' (With Philip Noël-Baker) British Committee for European Security and Cooperation, 1978

'Towards a New World Order. What does the Future Hold for me...' Liberation, 1978

Index

166